CONTENTS

ABOUT THIS BOOK – PLEASE READ!

This is **not** a textbook. By the time you read this, you should already have covered the whole syllabus and have attempted some examination-style questions. This guide will give you a solid outline of all the material in the Higher Economics Syllabus, but it should be used in conjunction with your experiences in class, your own notes, your textbooks, and past papers.

In this guide the emphasis is on subject knowledge, the structure of that knowledge, and how to answer examination questions. The final exam is not only a test of knowledge, but also a test of how you use economic theories and concepts to solve economic questions and problems. A good candidate will therefore see the contents of this book more as a toolkit with which they can successfully tackle the questions with which they are faced and maximise their exam mark. At the end of each section there are sample IB-style questions for you to put this approach into practice. The model markschemes for these questions are in the final section of the guide so that you can attempt the questions as you progress through each section and then check your efforts by turning to the back of the guide. All successful candidates will have attempted as many past papers and examination-style questions as possible. It is the most efficient and effective way to test the knowledge you are consolidating in your revision programme.

Key terms are printed in **bold type** and definitions are signalled by *italicised type*.

This guide contains a considerable number of diagrams, and I make no apologies for this! Whilst I might have had to be economical with the explanation of some ideas, diagrams could not be sacrificed. **They are central to all aspects of the examination**. You will be asked questions about diagrams, and any good candidate will be expected to use diagrams to illustrate their work.

Each page is printed with a wide margin. As I go through each area of the syllabus I have highlighted key exam skills and hints relevant to that particular area in this margin. Although the numerical questions in the Higher Level Paper 3 are covered in a separate OSC Guide by George Graves, I will indicate the numerical skills needed for each section of the syllabus.

Please feel free to email me at OSC@OSC-IB.com with any feedback, so later editions of this guide may be revised to improve the help given to candidates.

Best of luck for your revision!

Stephen Holroyd

SECTION 1: MICROECONOMICS

SCARCITY

The basic economic problem is **scarcity**. But, to be more accurate, the problem is **finite resources** (land, labour, capital and enterprise) in relation to **infinite wants**. Because these resources are finite, individual consumers, firms and governments constantly have to make **choices** between having one thing, and not having another. These choices can be focused down into three questions.

> What to produce?
> How to produce?
> For whom to produce?

All economies, whether tending to command or to free market, exist as an attempted solution to these three questions. All economies, including developed and less economically developed, face the same problem, and therefore the same questions. For example, developed economies might face the choice between more nuclear weapons or more healthcare, whereas a less economically developed country (ELDC) might face a choice between clean water and basic vaccination programmes.

Factors of Production are *the scarce resources that an economy has at its disposal to produce goods and services.*

> **Land** represents natural resources
> **Labour** is the human resource
> **Capital** is goods that are used to produce other goods, and requires an economy to forgo current consumption
> **Enterprise**, also a human resource, organises the three other factors to produce goods and services. The reward for this risky activity is **profit**

> It is important that you understand that the act of investment involves the buying of capital goods and has nothing to do with money.

Allocation of these resources can be organised through several different **Economic Systems**. In the end, all economies are **mixed**, although some will tend towards **free market** (eg. UK, USA), and others will tend towards **centrally-planned** or **command** (North Korea, Cuba). **Traditional** systems still exist in many of the poorest LDCs, and involve actions such as barter, gift and communal activities.

Opportunity Cost is *the cost of the next best thing forgone.* As long as economic resources are used in the production of a good or service, a cost is involved, even if a price is not.

A **Production Possibility Curve** (also referred to as boundary, or frontier) shows *the combinations of two goods/services that can be produced efficiently with a given set of resources:*

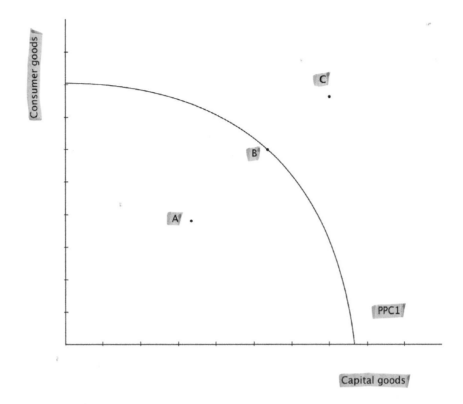

You will normally see a curved PPC, because as more consumer goods are produced, more capital goods have to be given up in order to produce each marginal unit of consumer goods. As we shall see later on, this is due to the **law of diminishing returns**.

Any combination of goods produced within the PPC (A) means that there are unemployed resources. Points on the PPC (B) represent different bundles of goods, but with fully employed resources. Points beyond the PPC (C) are currently unattainable. In order to attain these points, an economy would have to increase the number of resources, increase the productivity (efficiency) of its current resources, or improve technology. For example, Brazil discovers offshore oil, a developed economy invests in its human capital, and car factories become robotised.

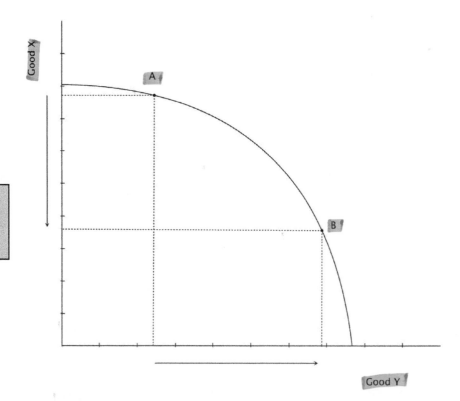

You should use arrows or actual numbers to show clearly that you understand the concept of Opportunity Cost in an exam.

As this economy moves from a combination of goods X and Y represented by A to a combination represented by B, the increase in the production of Y results in a reduction in the production of X. The opportunity cost of increasing Y is the forgone production of X.

A **shift in the PPC** represents an improvement in productivity and efficiency, or an increase in the quality and/or quantity of resources. It also represents economic growth.

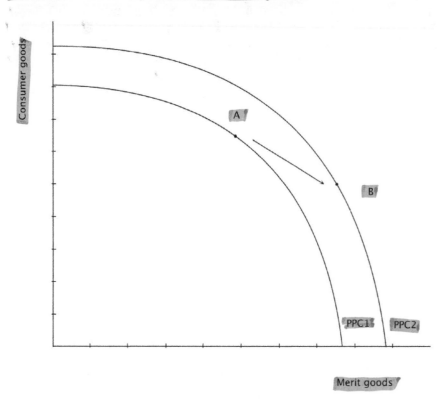

The PPC above shows an economy that is both growing and developing. The PPC has moved outwards and the production of merit goods has increased.

Some other important fundamental concepts that you need to know are:

Positive and normative statements. Positive economic statements are *objective*, and therefore can be tested by available evidence. Normative statements are *subjective* and express an opinion. These statements often contain the words 'should', 'could' or 'would'. For example, 'governments should ban smoking in public places' is a normative statement, whereas 'unemployment is higher this year than last year' is a positive statement.

Whether goods are **economic goods** or **free goods**. This depends upon whether they are scarce or not. Free goods are not scarce (they have no opportunity cost), and therefore have no market price. Economic goods are scarce.

Utility, which is *the satisfaction or pleasure gained from an economic action.* For a consumer, this is the satisfaction gained from consuming a product, and it is usually assumed that as more goods and services are consumed, the extra utility gained from consuming one more unit (marginal utility) will diminish.

MARKETS

A **market** is *a place where buyers (**demand**) and sellers (**supply**) meet to exchange goods or services at the market-clearing price.* Prices are determined in a free market solely by the interaction of demand and supply. As we shall see later on, governments can and do intervene to influence both price and output, and therefore the **allocation of resources**.

> You cannot avoid knowing about this most important area of syllabus areas. You MUST expect it to be tested in all three papers on markets, how they work, how governments intervene in them and how they fail.

Demand

Effective demand is *a want (quantity of goods/services) backed by the willingness and ability to buy at a given price.* Other things being equal, more will be demanded at lower prices than at higher prices, and so there will be an inverse relationship between price and quantity.

> Other things being equal, or *ceteris paribus*, is an important assumption made by economists so that they can isolate the effect of a single variable on something else.

- **Movement along the demand curve (extension/ contraction)**

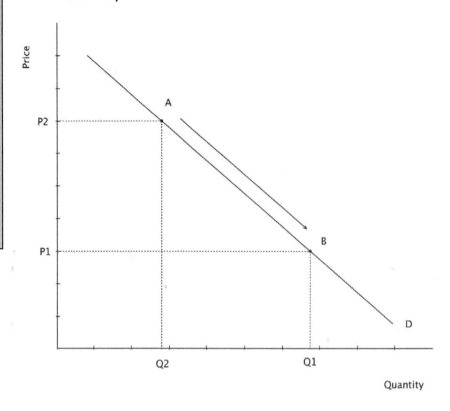

A change in the price of the good itself will cause a movement along the demand curve, and therefore change the quantity demanded. In the diagram above, a fall in price from P_2 to P_1 will cause an increase in the quantity demanded from Q_2 to Q_1, and an increase in price from P_1 to P_2 will cause a fall in the quantity demanded from Q_1 to Q_2. The relationship between the price change and the resultant quantity change will be explored later on when we look at **price elasticity of demand**.

A demand curve is downward sloping for two reasons:

> The **income effect**. *As prices fall, so real income increases.* Consumers can therefore afford to consume a greater quantity.
> The **substitution effect**. *As a good falls in price it becomes cheaper in relation to other goods* (substitutes).

- **Movement of the demand curve**

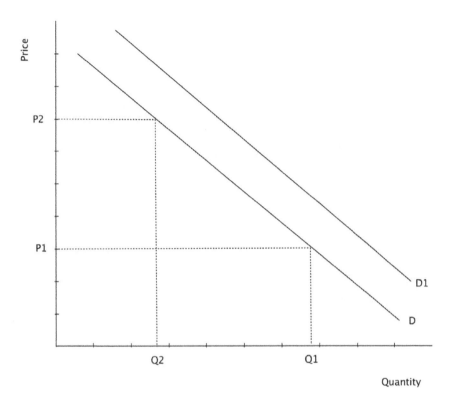

The following factors will cause a movement in the demand curve itself:

Income. For normal goods, an increase in income will cause an increase in demand (a shift of the demand curve to the right). For inferior goods, an increase in income will cause a fall in demand (a shift of the demand curve to the left).

A change in the distribution of income will also change the pattern of demand.

> Normal and inferior goods will be explained in detail when looking at income elasticity of demand.

Population. As population increases, the demand for most goods will increase. A change in the distribution of population will also have an effect. Thus, an ageing population has increased the demand for healthcare.

Price of complements. Goods and services are often consumed together, and are thus said to be in **joint demand**, for example, cars and petrol. An increase in the price of cars (leading to a fall in the quantity demanded of cars) will lead to a fall in the demand for petrol.

Price of substitutes. Many goods and services can be consumed as alternatives to other goods and services, and are thus said to be in **competitive demand**. An increase in the price of foreign holidays will lead to an increase in the demand for domestic holidays.

Tastes and preferences. These change frequently. There has been a great increase in the demand for organic food products in recent years. Of course, individuals' tastes and preferences are affected by advertising and marketing.

Supply

Supply is *the quantity of a good or service producers are able and willing to supply to a market at a given price.* An increase in price will usually lead to an increase in the quantity supplied, and thus there is a positive relationship between price and supply.

- **Movement along the supply curve (extension/ contraction)**

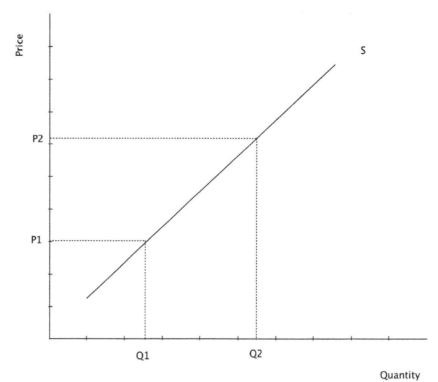

In the diagram above, a fall in price from P_2 to P_1 will cause a fall in the quantity supplied from Q to Q_1 (contraction), and an increase in price from P to P_2 will cause a rise in the quantity supplied from Q to Q_2 (expansion). Here, the changes in price will have been caused by a movement of the demand curve.

- **Movement of the supply curve**

The following factors will cause a movement of the supply curve itself:

> **Costs of production.** This is the key factor that shifts the supply curve. An increase in the price of factors of production will decrease supply, and a decrease in the price of factors of production will increase supply. An increase in the productivity of factors will increase supply.
>
> **Technology.** Technological advances reduce costs of production and so shift the supply curve to the right.

New firms entering a market. Any new firm that enters a market will increase market supply. This will be explored more when looking at **perfect competition**.

Indirect taxes and subsidies. Taxes will decrease supply, and subsides will increase supply.

Price of substitutes. A rise in the price of apples will encourage fruit growers to move from growing pears etc. to producing apples, and thus the supply of pears will decrease.

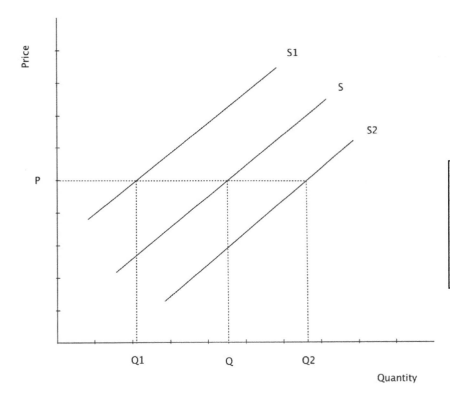

Questions quite often ask candidates to comment upon the determinants of demand and supply. If you know your determinants, these are very simple questions on which to score high marks.

Here S to S_1 represents a decrease in supply, and S to S_2 represents an increase in supply.

Equilibrium: the interaction of demand and supply

Equilibrium *exists when demand equals supply* (P,Q). **Disequilibrium** exists if there is a situation of excess demand (at Pa) or excess supply (at Pb) as shown below:

Examination questions in all three papers frequently ask candidates to illustrate, explain and analyse price changes, and a flexible knowledge of the determinants of demand and supply and the forces that lead to equilibrium is something that any successful candidate must have. You should see the determinants of demand and supply as flexible tools that you can apply to any market (house prices, oil prices and commodity prices) to explain price movements.

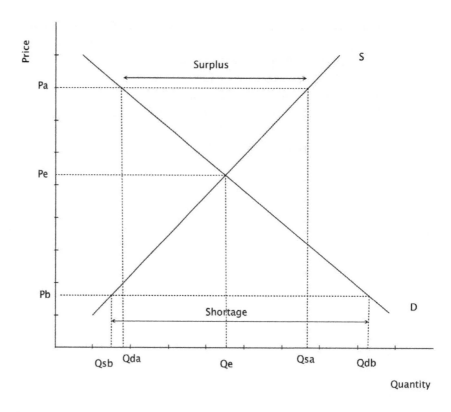

The equilibrium price is also known as the **market-clearing price**, as all the surpluses and excesses are cleared from the market and the forces of demand and supply are not acting to change this equilibrium. If disequilibrium exists, then the forces of demand and supply will automatically adjust the market to equilibrium. With excess demand, prices will be forced upwards due to the shortage that exists, and with excess supply, prices will be forced downwards due to the surplus that exists:

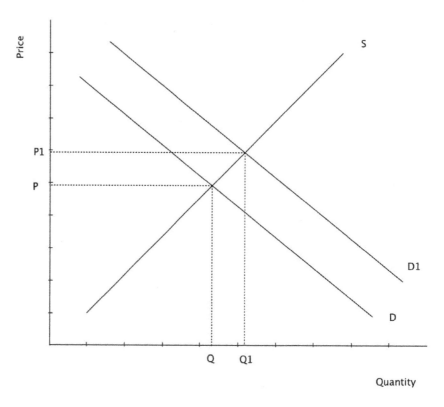

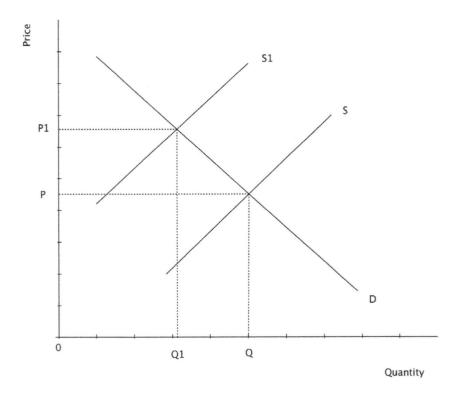

In a free market, a change in price can only be caused by changes in demand and/or supply, and nothing else. An increase in price can be caused either by an increase in demand or a decrease in supply. A fall in price can be caused either by a fall in demand or an increase in supply, as shown in the two diagrams above.

Numerical application:
Linear demand function ($Qd = a - bP$)
Linear supply function ($Qs = c + dP$)
Calculate equilibrium and excess demand/ supply
Plot, identify slope and horizontal intercept, and shift curves

---

● **The Role of the Price Mechanism**
Prices act as a **signal**, an **incentive** and a **rationing** device and the price mechanism helps to allocate resources. For example, if the demand for a product rises, then its price will rise, signalling to producers that consumers want to buy more of this good. The rising profits (from rising prices and rising consumption) will incentivise firms to produce more. As goods become scarce, their rising prices will ration their consumption.

Market Efficiency

Concepts of allocative efficiency, productive efficiency and Pareto optimality will be covered in detail under the heading of Market Structures.

- ## Consumer and Producer Surplus

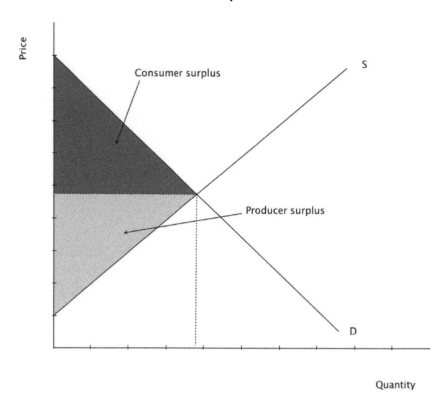

Consumer surplus is *the extra utility, over and above the price paid, gained by consumers.* **Producer surplus** is *the extra revenue gained by producers, over and above the price that the producer would need to be paid to produce that unit of output.* The sum of these two surpluses is known as community surplus (the total benefit to society). The increase or decrease of either of these two 'surpluses' and the movement of a 'surplus' from one stakeholder to another or even the disappearance of a 'surplus' are important ways of illustrating benefits or losses from economic events, and will be used widely later on in this Guide (see Market Failure, Trade Barriers).

Many students have major problems with the topic of elasticity. They frequently see it as an isolated topic and an excuse for examiners to ask questions that involve numbers. The concept of elasticity is immensely important for economists, as it enables us more accurately to picture, analyse and evaluate what goes on in the real world. Without PED and PES our demand and supply analysis would not be half as effective.

ELASTICITIES OF DEMAND AND SUPPLY

Elasticity *measures the responsiveness of one variable to a change in another.*

Price Elasticity of Demand

Price Elasticity of Demand (PED) measures *the responsiveness of the quantity demanded to a change in price.*

$$\text{PED} = \frac{\text{\% change in quantity demanded}}{\text{\% change in price}}$$

An alternative formula which is very useful is

$$\text{PED} = \frac{\Delta Q/Q}{\Delta P/P}$$

where ΔQ is the change in quantity demanded, Q is the original quantity, ΔP is the change in price, and P is the original price.

The calculation of PED results in a coefficient, or real number, and this tells us two major things about the responsiveness of the quantity demanded to a change in price.

Sign (positive or negative) gives information about the direction of the relationship. For all **Normal goods**, PED will be negative, as there is a negative relationship between price and quantity on a downward-sloping demand curve. We always ignore this negative sign. If PED is positive, then we have a perverse demand curve.

Magnitude. The size of the number resulting from the elasticity calculation tells us about the degree of response. The bigger the number, the bigger the response, and vice versa.

PED >1 means the good is price elastic
PED < 1 means the good is price inelastic
PED = 1 means the good has unit elasticity
PED = 0 means the good is perfectly price inelastic
PED = ∞ means the good is perfectly price elastic

Price elastic means that *the quantity demanded is highly responsive to a change in price*. In the diagram below a change in price from P_1 to P_2 results in a proportionately large response in the quantity demanded from Q_1 to Q_2:

Students should always look to comment on elasticity wherever they can. They should carefully consider whether they can use their knowledge of PED and PES to draw demand and supply curves which accurately reflect the market situation. For example, diagrams to illustrate agricultural and commodity markets should always have price inelastic demand and supply curves.

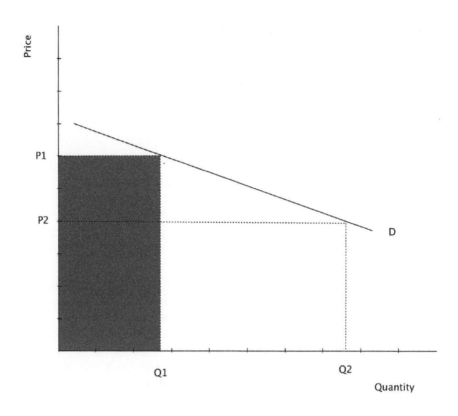

Price inelastic means that *the quantity demanded is highly unresponsive to a change in price.* In the diagram below a change in price from P_1 to P_2 results in a proportionately small response in the quantity demanded from Q_1 to Q_2:

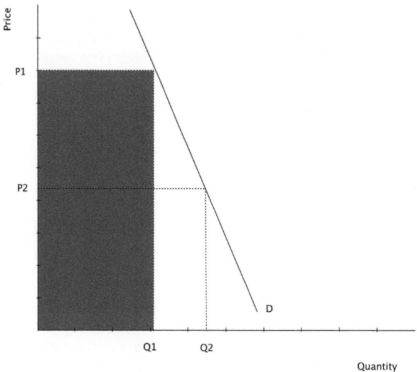

PED varies at every point along a straight-line demand curve.
PED is not the same as the gradient.
At high prices, PED tends towards infinity.

At low prices, PED tends towards zero.
At the mid-point PED = 1:

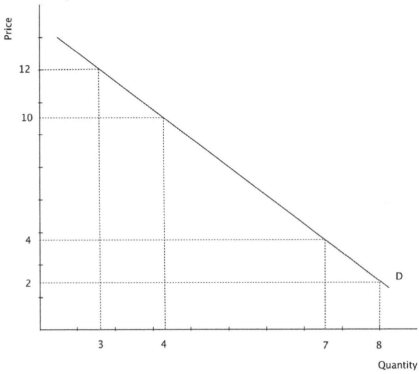

As price increases from 10 to 12:

$$\frac{-1/4}{+2/10} = (-)\ 1.25$$

As price increases from 2 to 4:

$$\frac{-1/8}{+2/2} = (-)\ 0.125$$

- **Determinants of PED**

    Closeness of substitutes. PED will be more price elastic
    if there are close substitutes available.
    Luxury or necessity. Luxury goods tend to be price
    elastic, and necessities tend to be price inelastic.
    Percentage of income spent on the good. The smaller
    the percentage of income spent on a good, the more price
    inelastic demand will be.
    Time period. In the long run, demand tends to be more
    price elastic, as it takes time for consumers to react to price
    changes.

- **PED of Commodities and Manufactured Goods**

Demand for commodities tends to be price inelastic as they are
necessities and have few substitutes. Therefore, any change in
the supply of commodities will cause wide fluctuation in prices. On
the other hand, manufactured goods with more substitutes tend to
have price elastic demand curves, and thus supply-side
fluctuations will cause less substantial changes in prices.

> PED will appear again when we
> look at price discrimination, and
> the effects of a depreciation in
> the exchange rate on the
> balance of payments.

- **PED and Total Revenue (TR)**

$$TR = P \times Q$$

Total revenue is a useful way to check the PED of a demand curve. If a rise in price causes total revenue to increase, then PED is inelastic. If an increase in price causes total revenue to decrease, then the demand curve is price elastic. If an increase in price causes total revenue to increase then the demand curve is price inelastic. If a change in price does not change total revenue, the PED is unitary (= 1).

In the diagrams on page 16, TR at $P_2 = P_2 \times Q_2$. After an increase in price, TR at $P_1 = P_1 \times Q_1$ (shaded area).

Cross Price Elasticity of Demand

You should see the link between XED and the price of other goods, which was compliments and substitutes as determinants of demand. A fall in the price of a complement will cause an increase in demand (a shift of the demand curve to the right) for the good that is in joint demand. A fall in the price of a substitute will cause a decrease in demand (a shift of the demand curve to the left) for the good that is in competitive demand.

Cross Price Elasticity of Demand (XED) measures *the responsiveness of the quantity demanded of one good to a change in price of another.*

$$XED = \frac{\text{\% change in quantity demanded good A}}{\text{\% change in price good B}}$$

An alternative formula which is very useful is

$$XED = \frac{\Delta Q_A / Q_A}{\Delta P_B / P_B}$$

where ΔQ_A is the change in quantity demanded of good A, Q_A is the original quantity of good A, ΔP_B is the change in price of good B, and P_B is the original price of good B.

Sign (positive or negative). **Substitutes** (*goods in competitive demand*) will have a positive XED. **Complements** (*goods in joint demand*) will have a negative XED.
Magnitude. The higher the value of XED the closer the relationship (either complement or substitute) will be between the two goods in question.

Income Elasticity of Demand

Income Elasticity of Demand (YED) measures *the responsiveness of the quantity demanded to a change in the real income of consumers.*

$$YED = \frac{\text{\% change in quantity demanded}}{\text{\% change in real income}}$$

An alternative formula which is very useful is

$$YED = \frac{\Delta Q/Q}{\Delta Y/Y}$$

where ΔQ is the change in quantity demanded, Q is the original quantity, ΔY is the change in income, and Y is the original income.

> **Sign** (positive or negative). Positive means that the good is a **normal good** (*as income increases, so will the quantity demanded*). Here an increase in income will result in the demand curve shifting to the right. Negative means that the good is an **inferior good** (*as income increases, so the quantity demanded will fall*). Here an increase in income will result in the demand curve shifting to the left.
> **Magnitude**. The higher the value of YED the closer the relationship will be between a change in income and the change in the quantity demanded (0-1 being necessities and 1-∞ being luxuries).

Price Elasticity of Supply

Price Elasticity of Supply (PES) measures *the responsiveness of the quantity supplied to a change in price.*

$$PES = \frac{\%\ change\ in\ quantity\ supplied}{\%\ change\ in\ price}$$

An alternative formula which is very useful is

$$PES = \frac{\Delta Qs/Qs}{\Delta P/P}$$

where ΔQs is the change in quantity supplied, Qs is the original quantity supplied, ΔP is the change in price, and P is the original price.

> **Sign** (positive or negative). Supply curves have a positive PES.
> **Magnitude**. The size of the number resulting from the elasticity calculation tells us about the degree of response. The bigger the number, the bigger the response, and vice versa.

> > PES >1 means the good is price elastic.
> > PES < 1 means the good is price inelastic.
> > PES = 1 means the good has unit elasticity (any curve from the origin).
> > PES = 0 means the good is perfectly price inelastic.
> > PES = ∞ means the good is perfectly price elastic.

Questions quite often ask candidates to comment upon the determinants of PED and PES. If you know your determinants, these are very simple questions on which to score high marks.

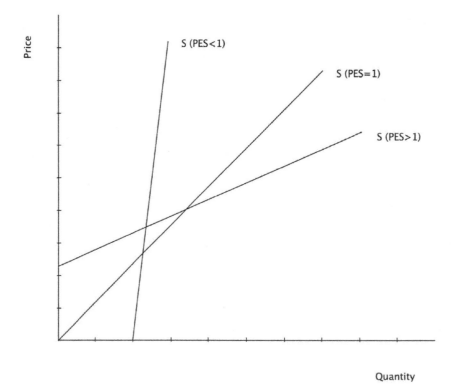

- **Determinants of PES**

  Time period. In the very short run all factors are fixed, and therefore PES = 0. In the short run at least one factor is fixed and at least one factor is variable, and therefore PES = <1. In the long run all factors are variable (except technology), and PES >1.

  Level of spare capacity. If firms are at full capacity the supply curve will be price inelastic. The more spare capacity the more price elastic the supply curve will be.

  Type of Good. For some goods there are time lags in production. This is particularly true in agricultural markets. Supply may be perfectly price inelastic in the very short run

  Level of stocks. If firms are in the habit of keeping high stock levels, they will easily be able to respond to changes in demand, and therefore supply will be price elastic.

- **PES of Commodities and Manufactured Goods**

Supply of commodities tends to be price inelastic as it takes time for producers to respond to increases in demand given that not all factors are variable (many commodities have growing seasons). Manufactured goods tend to have a price elastic supply, as there are not the same time-lags in production.

Price inelastic supply combined with price inelastic demand for commodities means that any changes in demand or supply lead to considerable fluctuations in prices. The volatility of commodity prices makes commodity producers vulnerable to fluctuations in income (the major source of investment).

Numerical application:
Calculate PED, XED, YED and PES
Sign and magnitude
Application and implication for stakeholders

GOVERNMENT INTERVENTION

Governments intervene in markets because they believe that the equilibrium reached by the free market is not desirable. In other words, they believe that price and/or quantity are in the wrong place. Thus they employ a variety of methods to move both price and quantity. For example, most governments believe that the free market equilibrium price of cigarettes would be too low and therefore they tax them. Of course, there are issues of market failure involved here.

> It is important that you see the links between government intervention in the market, price elasticity of demand and supply, and market failure.

Maximum and Minimum Prices

A **maximum price** is also known as a **price ceiling**, and to be effective it must be set *below* the market-clearing price.

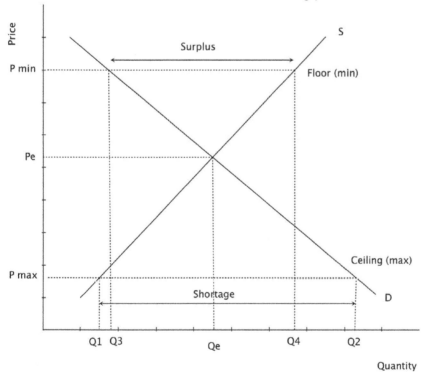

A maximum price will result in a shortage or excess demand (Q1 to Q2), with consumers benefitting from lower prices. However, often a **parallel** market will evolve. To cure this problem, a government might have to introduce **rationing**, or, as in the graph below, the government could attempt to shift the supply curve by using subsidies, producing themselves, or releasing stocks of previously produced goods into the market.

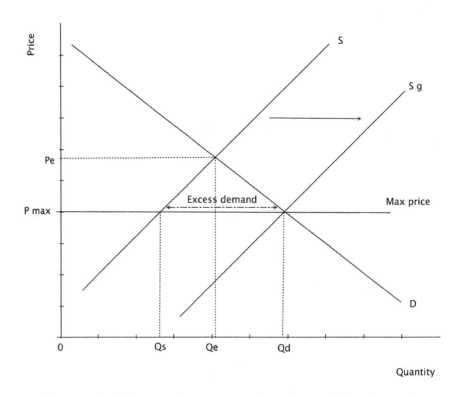

A **minimum price**, also known as a **price floor**, must be set *above* the equilibrium price to be effective. A classic example of a minimum price is minimum wage legislation, resulting in a surplus Q3 to Q4 (this would be unemployment in a labour market). A minimum price will raise or protect incomes for producers and a minimum wage will protect incomes for workers. However, both create excess supply, and here the government can intervene to increase demand, as in the graph below. This it can do by buying the surplus at the minimum price, which then must be stored, sold in alternative markets, or simply destroyed.

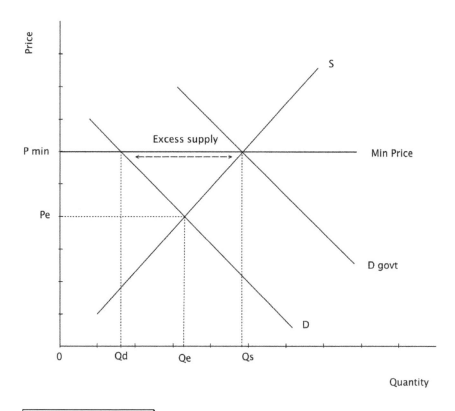

Indirect taxation

Indirect taxes are taxes on expenditure. As these increase a firm's costs of production, they will move the supply curve upwards to the left. If the tax is a **specific** tax (*a fixed monetary amount on each unit of output*, for example four pence on a litre of petrol), the supply curve shift will be a parallel shift. If the tax is an **ad valorem** tax (*a percentage tax*, for example 20% VAT in the UK), the new supply curve will gradually diverge from the original.

As the text increases costs of production, it will reduce supply. Although the tax is imposed on producers, some of the burden of the tax can be passed on to consumers. The final balance of the burden (between consumers and producers) will depend upon the price elasticity of demand and the price elasticity of supply for the good or service.

In the next graph, with a price inelastic demand curve, the producer finds it relatively easy to pass the tax onto the consumer. The tax per unit is represented by the vertical distance between the two supply curves. The total tax revenue is equal to the tax per unit multiplied by the equilibrium quantity (0 to QT). Here the tax has a relatively small effect on the equilibrium quantity.

> It is important to be able both to analyse and evaluate the effects of the various methods of government intervention. An average candidate will simply state the effects. A good candidate will comment on how effective the measures are, and the wider implications. For example, in the diagram on the next page, a good candidate would comment that the tax does not reduce equilibrium quantity very much, and that the consumer pays most of the burden of taxation.

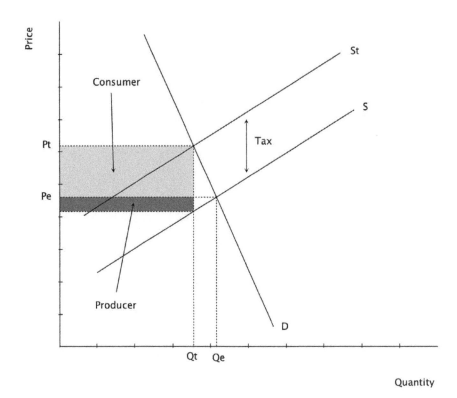

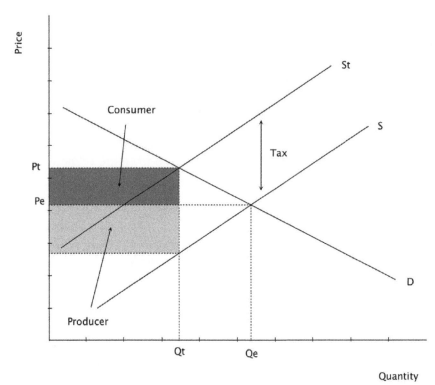

Here, in the graph above, the producer finds it relatively difficult to pass the tax onto the consumer.

The consumer will carry the greater tax burden if price elasticity of demand is inelastic, or price elasticity of supply is elastic. The producer will carry the greater tax burden if price elasticity of demand is elastic, or price elasticity of supply is inelastic.

Subsidies

Subsidies are *payments by a government to producers.* They reduce the costs of production and increase output. As they reduce the costs of production they will shift the supply curve downwards to the right. They will have the effect of increasing the price the producer receives for each unit of output (Pe to Pp in the diagram below), and reducing the price the consumer pays for each unit consumed (Pe to Pc). The total cost of the subsidy, to the government, is Pp to Pc multiplied by 0 to Qs (area a+b+c+d+e+f).

Before the subsidy consumer spending was f+e+g. After the subsidy consumer spending is g+i+j for an increased quantity.

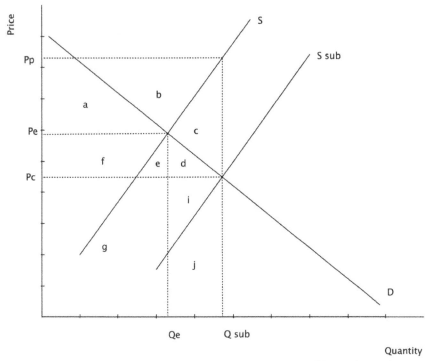

The increase in producer revenue is a+b+c+d+i+j (from f+e+g).

It is important that you can discuss the consequences of all these forms of government intervention for the stakeholders in the market (consumers, producers and the government). In order to do this you should look to comment on consumers and producer surplus, producer revenue, government revenue and expenditure as well as the actual impacts on the equilibrium price and quantity.

Numerical application:
Plot demand and supply curves
New supply curves for taxes and subsidies
New equilibria
Calculate changes in consumer expenditure, producer revenue, tax revenue, government expenditure, tax incidence (burden), total subsidy per unit, excess demand, excess supply

---

MARKET STRUCTURES

Aims and Objectives of Firms

Profit maximisation dominates this section. You need, however, to understand where a firm might maximise sales revenue/total revenue.

There is a wide range of possible aims and objectives for firms to target, including sales revenue maximisation, output maximisation, managerial goals, behavioural goals, market share and satisfising, but underpinning much of the theory in this section is the aim of **profit maximisation**.

Profit = total revenue – total cost

Total revenue = price x quantity

Total cost = average cost x quantity

(Or fixed costs + variable costs)

To understand effectively how a firm works, you need to understand costs and revenue in some detail.

Production and Costs

• Costs in the Short Run

$TC = FC + VC$
$ATC = TC / Q$
$ATC = AFC + AVC$
$AFC = FC / Q$
$AVC = VC / Q$
$MC = \Delta TC / \Delta Q$
MC = the slope of TC

A **firm** is *a combination of the four factors of production*. These four factors are transformed into output. As these factors must be paid for, production incurs costs.

In the **short run**, *at least one factor is variable, and at least one factor is fixed*. Even though the firm's size is fixed, increasing amounts of a variable factor (eg. labour) can be added to the firm.

Here the **law of diminishing returns** applies. This law states that *as successive units of the variable factor are added, the extra (marginal) output produced will at first increase and then decrease.* This results in the marginal product (MP) and average product (AP) curves below:

Questions asking you to distinguish between short and long run costs do appear in the essay paper (part a), but elsewhere all you will be required to do is to draw your cost curves accurately, and in combination with revenue curves, analyse the behaviour of firms.

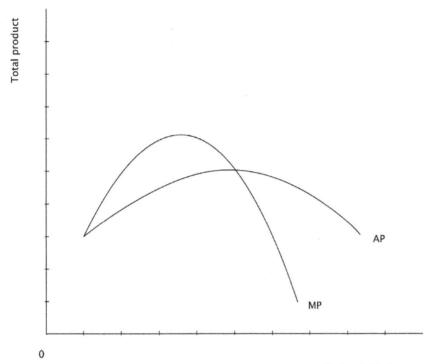

Of course, each time a unit of the variable factor is added, a new cost is incurred. If this new cost allows output first to increase and then decrease, the marginal costs and average variable costs must first decrease and then increase. This results in the **marginal cost** (MC) and **average variable cost** (AVC) curves below. Marginal cost is *the cost of producing one extra unit of output*:

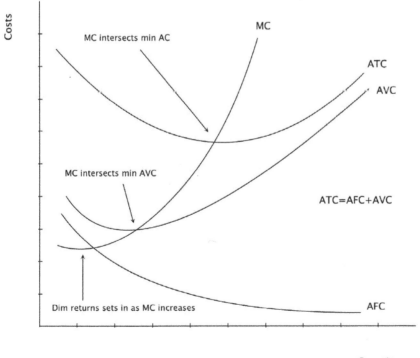

Fixed costs are *the cost of producing nothing*, and so average fixed costs (AFC) fall as output increases. **Total costs** are *the sum of fixed and variable costs*, and so **average total costs** are *the sum of average fixed costs and average variable costs*. In the diagram above, ATC is created by adding the AVC and AFC lines together.

Economic costs of production are divided into two types of costs. **Explicit costs** are the monetary payments (wages etc) to factors of production not already owned by a firm. **Implicit costs** (normal profit) are those faced by a firm forgoing what it could have earned by employing its factors in another activity (opportunity cost).

● **Costs in the Long Run**

In the **long run**, *all factors are variable*, and therefore a firm can change its size (scale).

If a firm increases its size, then one of three things can happen to output:

> 1) Output can increase more than proportionately (increasing returns to scale).
> 2) Output can increase proportionately (constant returns to scale).
> 3) Output can increase less than proportionately (decreasing returns to scale).

1) will cause average costs to fall, 2) will cause average costs to remain constant, and 3) will cause average costs to rise, resulting in the long run average cost curve below.

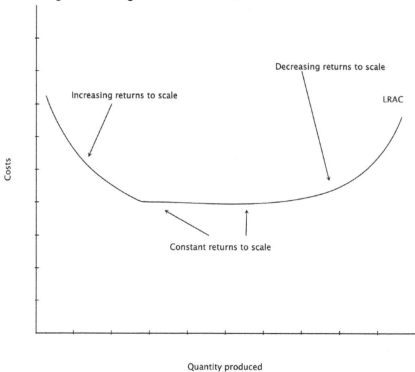

LRAC is the 'envelope' curve of all SRACs that make up the short run.

It is **economies of scale** that cause average costs to fall in the long run, and **diseconomies of scale** that cause average costs to rise in the long run.

Economies of scale can be divided into the following categories:

- Financial economies
- Marketing economies
- Technical economies
- Purchasing economies
- Managerial economies

Diseconomies of scale tend to be very firm specific, but can be divided into the following categories:

- Communication issues
- Alienation and firm politics
- Increased regulation from government

Revenue

The shape of a firm's revenue curves (AR, MR, TR) depends upon whether the firm is in perfect or imperfect competition.

In **perfect competition** the firm is a price taker. Price is constant, and therefore the following revenue curves are generated:

$TR = P \times Q$
$AR = TR / Q$
AR therefore $= P$
$MR = \Delta TR / \Delta Q$
MR = the slope of TR

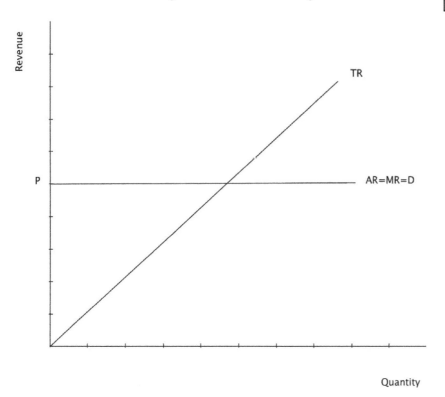

TR is a straight line because MR is constant.

In **imperfect competition** the firm is a price maker, and so it can influence the price at which its goods sell, or the number of goods which it sells. It thus faces a normal downward-sloping demand curve. As the demand curve shows us price/quantity demanded combinations, it also shows us AR.

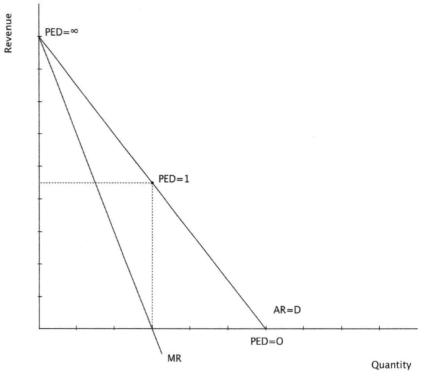

As AR is downward sloping, MR must be falling below it. When MR = 0, PED = 1.

As MR is the slope of TR, TR will rise at a declining rate. When MR cuts the quantity axis, total revenue will cease to rise, as MR = 0. As MR becomes negative, TR will fall. When MR = 0, TR is maximised.

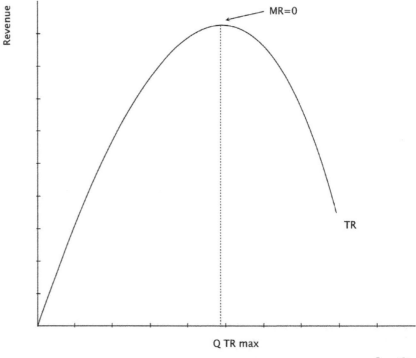

As shown above, PED varies all the way along a straight-line demand curve. At the mid-point, PED = 1, and this coincides with MR = 0. When MR = 0, total revenue (sales revenue) is also maximised.

Profit

Economic profit is different from **accounting profit**.

Profit = TR – TC (implicit and explicit costs)
Profit = (AR x Q) – (AC x Q)
Profit = Q (AR – AC)

TR = TC results in **normal profit**.
TR > TC results in **supernormal/abnormal profit**.
TR < TC results in losses.

Profit maximisation involves maximising the degree to which TR > TC. Firms will want to produce every single good that contributes more to total revenue (MR) than it contributes to total costs (MC). A profit maximising firm will therefore produce every single good with an MR greater than its MC.

The diagram below uses the revenue curves from a perfectly competitive firm, however, the profit maximising condition is the same for imperfectly competitive firms with downward sloping revenue curves.

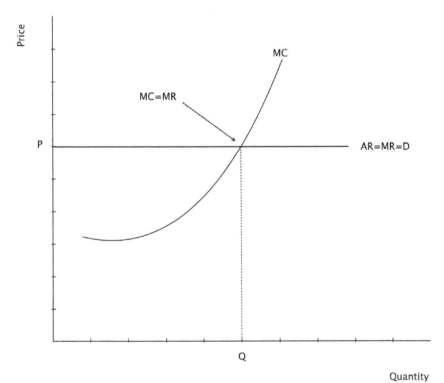

A firm should keep increasing its output as long as MR is greater than MC, and so **profit maximising equilibrium** is where **MC = MR**.

Perfect Competition

Although unlikely to exist, perfect competition provides an essential theoretical benchmark with which to compare other, less perfect, forms of competition. It illustrates the perfect working of the price mechanism. It is based on the following assumptions:

- Perfect knowledge
- A large number of small firms
- Freedom of entry and exit
- Homogeneous product
- Profit maximisation

Because of these assumptions, firms are **price takers** from the market equilibrium. Firms cannot sell at a higher price and would be irrational to sell at a lower price, as they would not sell a greater quantity:

Although the diagrams might look daunting, it is important to be able to use perfect competition as a way of illustrating how a free market can lead to economic efficiency. It is also an important tool with which to evaluate monopoly, and IB questions often link perfect competition and monopoly together, with good answers requiring strong diagrammatical analysis.

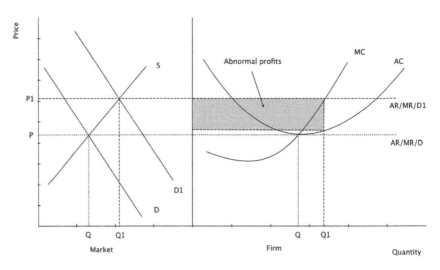

Profit maximisation is where MC = MR. The firm starts in equilibrium at P, Q. An increase in demand in the market increases the market price to P_1, and so the firm now takes a new price at P_1 with the equilibrium output level at Q_1. Because AR > AC at output level Q_1 this firm is making supernormal profits. New firms are attracted by these profits and enter the market, thus increasing the market supply curve. As supply increases, price, and therefore profits, fall. New firms will continue to enter as long as supernormal profits are being made. But when price falls back to P normal profits are made, and the firm reaches long run equilibrium (P, Q).

If losses are being made in the short run firms/resources will leave the market, resulting in the market supply curve shifting to the left and prices rising. With the rising market prices firms will also increase prices, and so losses will decrease until long run equilibrium is reached at normal profit:

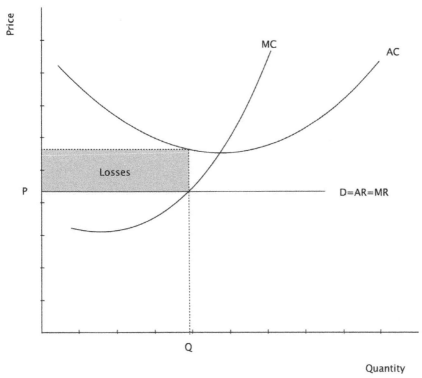

At long run equilibrium, P = Q = AR = MR = D = AC = MC, and here both **allocative** and **productive efficiency** are achieved.

Allocative efficiency is achieved when **price = marginal cost**.

Productive (technical) efficiency is achieved where **AC is at a minimum** (MC = AC).

Perfect competition is said to lead to a **Pareto optimal situation** where *the allocation of resources cannot be changed to make someone better off without making someone worse off.*
Here we have made the important assumption that there are no externalities in this market.

In perfect competition, the **MC curve is the firm's supply curve**. In the short run, this extends down towards the AVC curve. The **shut-down condition** is that *firms will stay in business as long as they are covering their variable costs.* But in the long run firms will only stay in business if they cover their average costs.

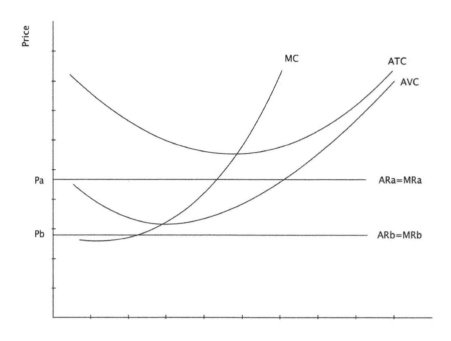

In the diagram above, the firm will stay in business at price Pa but shut down at price Pb.

Monopoly

A pure monopoly is a **single seller** (*a firm that produces 100% of market output*), although it is assumed that any firm with a market share in excess of 25% will have market power.

A monopoly market is characterised by a firm which is

- A single seller
- Produces branded goods
- Creates barriers to entry
- Maximises profits

As the firm is the market, the firm's revenue curves will be downward sloping. It is **barriers to entry** (economies of scale, legal barriers, sunk costs, capital costs, brand loyalty, control of inputs, predatory pricing and other aggressive tactics) that give a monopoly its **market power** (*the power to change price*).

The monopoly will maximise profits where MC = MR. P, Q is both the short-run and the long-run equilibrium, because barriers to entry stop new firms entering, and supernormal profits persist in the long run, as shown below. In the long run a monopoly produces at a point which is both allocatively and productively inefficient.

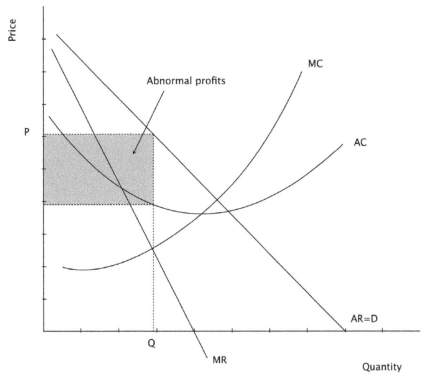

P > MC. Consumers are willing to pay a price higher than it costs to produce the product. In perfect competition, output would increase, so P = MC.

Q is not at minimum average cost. The monopoly is not using the most efficient combination of factors.

A monopoly is assumed to be "bad" because it is both allocatively and productively inefficient, and because it increases prices and reduces output.
A monopoly aiming to maximise total revenue will produce where MR = 0.
A monopoly aiming to maximise output will produce where AR = AC.
The diagram below illustrates different potential output levels for a monopolist, depending upon its goals.

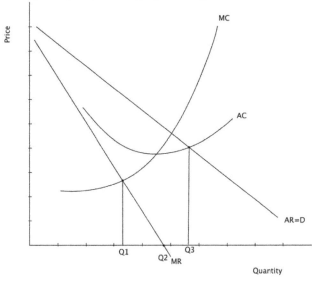

Q1: Profit maximisation (MC=MR)
Q2: Revenue maximisation (MR=0)
Q3: Output maximisation (AR=AC)

A **natural monopoly** exists when the costs of production are at their lowest, through economies of scale, when only one firm is in the market. Good examples are utility markets (electricity, gas and water).

With the minimum efficient scale of production at Q1 a single firm, operating efficiently, can supply all the market demand. If this market were to be split between two or more firms (Q2 and Q3) then the costs of production would rise:

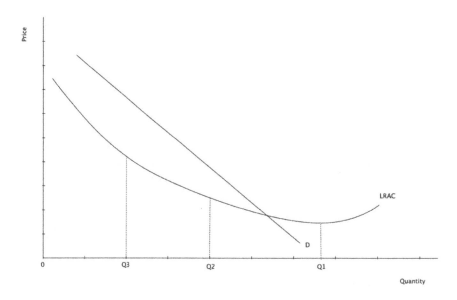

Perfect Competition and Monopoly Compared

> Candidates are frequently asked to compare perfect competition and imperfectly competitive structures in essay questions. If you can master a few diagrams and a clear structure it is an easy way of gaining good marks.

We have already seen that a monopoly is not allocatively and productively efficient, whereas perfect competition is. The diagrams below show that a monopoly will increase price (PM) compared to that of perfect competition (PPC), and reduce output (QM) compared to perfect competition (QPC). The shaded area represents welfare loss. Here we have generated a perfectly competitive equilibrium from the AR curve, because in perfect competition P = MC.

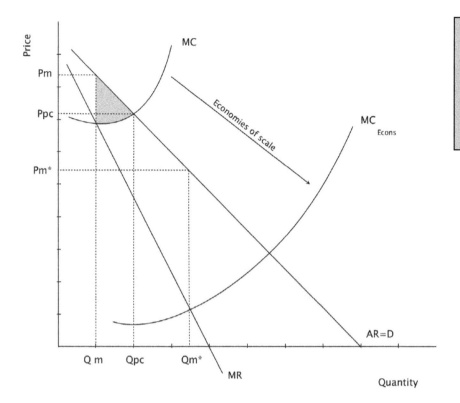

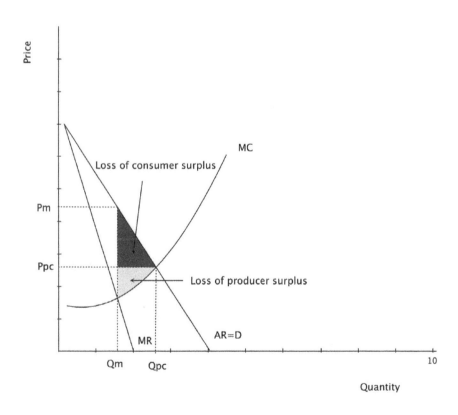

But this initial comparison using MC is flawed. We have assumed the same cost conditions for both firms, and a monopoly is likely to be able to benefit from **economies of scale**, thus reducing marginal costs to MC_{Econs}. If the monopoly can reduce marginal costs far enough, it might be able to produce a level of output Q_M* that is greater than Q_{PC} and reduce price P_M* below P_{PC}.

It is important that you are able to discuss firms in terms of their market power and their impact on efficiency.

A good candidate will be able to analyse and evaluate these concepts in a way which takes into account the impact a firm might have on different stakeholders.

There are other reasons why a monopoly may be beneficial:

- Supernormal profits may be used for Research and Development
- Monopolies may be beneficial for both employment and export, and tax revenues
- "Creative destruction"

Monopolistic Competition

Here the assumptions are now differentiated products, relatively free entry and exit for firms and a relatively large number of firms (in comparison to monopoly). Although the market is still very competitive, firms now have the ability to set prices. New firms are attracted by abnormal profits (as a shown in the diagram below) and so long-run equilibrium exists when only normal profits exist.

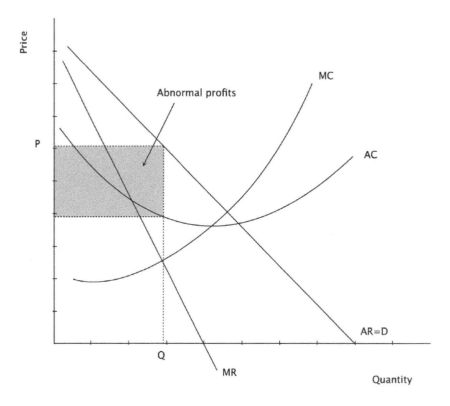

New firms enter (or leave), attracted by supernormal profits (or forced out by losses) and this causes the demand (AR) curve, of current firms, to fall (or rise) until long run equilibrium (normal profits when AR=AC) is reached.

Short-run losses:

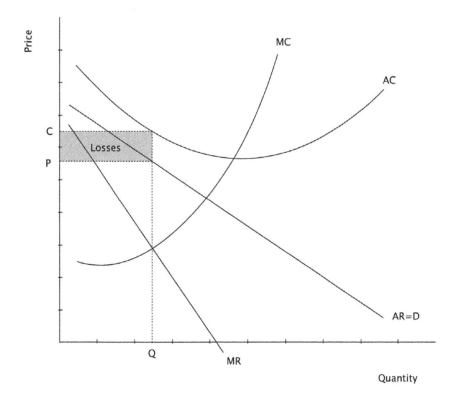

Long-run equilibrium:

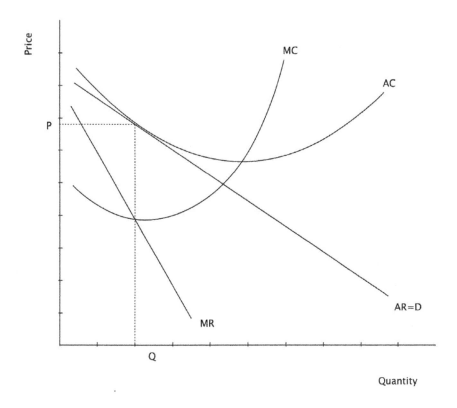

Good examples of monopolistically competitive markets are take-away food, hairdressing and book publishing.

Whilst firms in monopolistic competition are not allocatively and productively efficient, consumers can benefit from choice and non-price competition and firms can benefit from brand loyalty. Firms still only make abnormal profits in the short run and will not benefit from economies of scale, and the costs of non-price competition can be high.

Oligopoly

Whilst Kinked Demand Curve theory is the mainstay of oligopoly theory in the IB syllabus, you should not automatically respond to any oligopoly question with this theory. This important market structure deserves a more complete analysis, involving game theory and price leadership as an explanation of the interdependent behaviour of firms.

Oligopoly is the predominant existing market structure. *The market is dominated by a few large firms.* Significant barriers to entry exist. Economic theory seeks to explain why prices are 'sticky' but not why they exist in the first place, as in perfect competition or monopoly. Other oligopolistic characteristics are non-price competition, collusive behaviour and interdependence.

A **concentration ratio (CR)** quantifies the proportion of total market output that is held by a number of firms. A five-firm concentration ratio (CR5) is calculated by dividing the total output of the five largest firms in a given market by the aggregate output of that market. The larger the ratio the more concentrated the market and so the closer to monopoly. A CR of 50-80% (medium CR) would indicate an oligopolistic market and anything of 80% and above (high CR) would indicate a monopoly market.

Oligopoly models are divided into **collusive** and **non-collusive** models. If you are required to analyse/evaluate a collusive oligopoly then use the monopoly model as *this is when firms have a formal or informal ('tacit') agreement to limit competition and raise prices.* In non-collusive markets firms do not 'cooperate' and so they have to develop strategies to cope with their interdependence. Here the Kinked Demand Curve model, game theory and price leadership can be used to explain their behaviour.

The **Kinked Demand Curve** explains why, once a price is achieved, a firm will tend not to move from this price. This is because if a firm increases price, other firms will not follow, so the firm will lose total revenue (an increase in price leading to a fall in total revenue means the demand curve is price elastic). On the other hand, if the firm decides to reduce price, other firms will follow, and the firm will lose total revenue again (a decrease in price leading to a fall in total revenue means the demand curve is price inelastic). As the demand curve (AR) is kinked, two different MR curves are needed, and a discontinuous zone is formed. If the marginal cost curve varies within this zone, prices will still not change. If the MC curve moves out of this zone (MC_2) then P and Q will change:

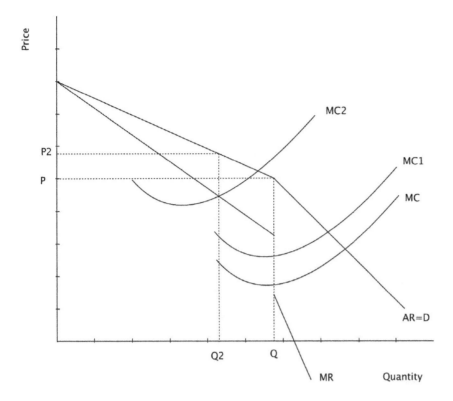

Game Theory explains interdependence. What is often called 'the prisoner's dilemma' illustrates the choices a firm faces when deciding whether to make a competitive change to price or to cooperate with rival firms.

		Firm X	
		$3.00	**$2.70**
Firm Y	**$3.00**	$15 mill each	$7.5 mill $18 mill
	$2.70	$18 mill $7.5 mill	$12 mill each

The box shows the outcomes of each firm's decision to change price. If Firm Y cuts its price from $3.00 to $2.70 and X does not follow, then Y's profits will rise to $18 mill and X's profits will fall to $7.5 mill. If firm X follows the cut in price both firms will experience a fall in their profits to $12 mill. If Y kept its price at $3.00 and firm X cut its price to $2.70, Y's profits would fall to $7.5 mill. This is the dominant strategy in this game. The safe option (maximin) is to cut price knowing that the other firm might follow and so the loss of profits is minimised. The more optimistic approach (maximax) is to cut price and hope that the other firm does *not* follow. Therefore the same strategy, cutting price, is followed in both approaches.

Price Leadership Models illustrate situations in which a single firm leads other firms in price-making decisions ('tacit' collusion). The leading firm changes price, and other firms follow. **Dominant** firm price leadership is where *the dominant firm in a market sets the price and other follow.* **Barometric** firm price leadership is where *the firm that others believe reflects market conditions most accurately sets the price and others follow.*

Price Discrimination

Throughout Market Structures you should be able to apply the concepts of productive and allocative efficiency, and illustrate them in diagrams when assessing different market structures.

Price discrimination occurs when *different consumers are charged different prices for the same good or service*. Firms price discriminate to turn consumer surplus into profit. There are three conditions which must exist for this to take place:

- A firm must have monopoly power
- There is no possibility of resale
- Different groups must be identified clearly

For example, students and pensioners often pay reduced rates for goods such as train tickets.

> **1st degree** price discrimination is when *firms charge consumers the maximum price they are willing to pay*.
> **2nd degree** price discrimination is when *firms charge different prices according to how much is consumed*.
> **3rd degree** price discrimination is when *a market is divided into two or more discrete markets each with its own price*. This is the most common form of price discrimination.

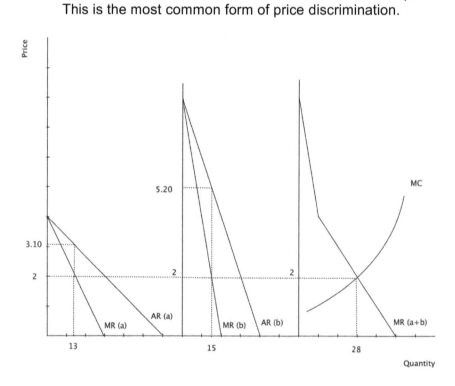

Here, the two discrete markets ('a' and 'b') are aggregated into (a+b) and the firm will profit maximise where the aggregate MR curve is equal to MC. This level of MC intersects MR in both discrete markets setting the profit maximising level in each market (13 in market 'a' and 15 in market 'b'). The price in market 'b' is higher than in market 'a' as it reflects the more price inelastic demand of these consumers.

For price discrimination to be effective, a firm must be a price maker, markets must be easily separated in terms of factors such as time and place, there must be no possibility of resale, and price elasticity of demand must differ in each individual market.

Firms able to price discriminate will benefit from an increase in total revenue. They may also be able to force competitive firms out of business, by cross-subsidising on markets (predatory pricing). Some consumers will benefit from the lower prices, and if profits are reinvested they will benefit from reinvestment and possible lower future costs.

Numerical application:
Calculate short-run shut-down price and break-even price
Calculate revenue max level of output

MARKET FAILURE AND GOVERNMENT RESPONSE

Market Failure is any situation when *the market mechanism fails to allocate scarce resources efficiently.* This is often seen as a rationale for government intervention. The main types of market failure are:

- **Negative and positive externalities of production and consumption**
- **Lack of public goods**
- **Merit and demerit goods**
- **Abuse of monopoly power**
- **Common access resources and sustainability**
- **Asymmetric information**

You should also be aware of **income and wealth inequality**.

> This is a very important part of the syllabus, and there are plenty of current real-world examples of market failure. Your exam **will** contain questions on market failure, particularly on the short answer and essay paper. When writing about market failure it is important that you are able to explain exactly **why** the market fails, and **analyse** the causes of these failures. Once failure has been explained, cures or responses should not only be listed and described, but **evaluated**. For each type of market failure, can you complete the sentence "the market fails because..."? If you use this sentence and successfully complete it in your answer, you will have shown your examiner that you can analyse the causes of market failure.

Externalities

Here the market fails because it *fails to measure the true costs or benefits of production or consumption.* **Externalities** are *the costs or benefits of production or consumption that are experienced by third parties, but not by the producers and consumers who cause them.*

Negative externalities

Classic examples of negative externalities are any form of pollution and traffic congestion. They are best illustrated as negative externalities from production (this will focus on the supply curve). Here, the market fails to measure the true costs of production to society. In a free market the supply curve measures the **marginal**

private cost (MPC), but it fails to measure the **marginal external cost** (MEC). The true cost to society, the **marginal social cost** (MSC), is equal to MPC + MEC. The shaded area is welfare loss:

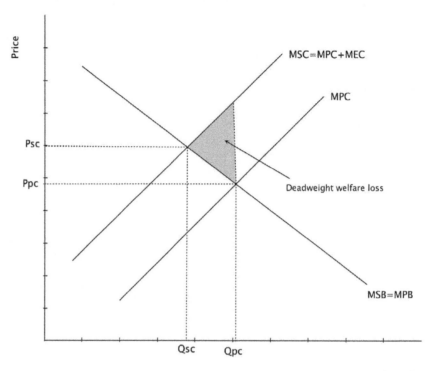

The free market equilibrium (where demand = supply, or marginal social benefit MSB = MPC), results in both over-production and over-consumption of the good or service. In the diagram above, this is output level QPC. If the market were to take into account the true costs of production, as shown by the MSC curve, then output would be at QSC (socially optimal level). So here the free market has failed to allocate resources efficiently, and has overproduced/consumed goods with negative spillover effects.

The shaded area represents the welfare loss to society created by this overproduction. In the diagram below, each good has a MSC that is greater than its MSB. In this example, we have assumed that there is no positive externality in consumption, and therefore marginal private benefits are equal to marginal social benefits.

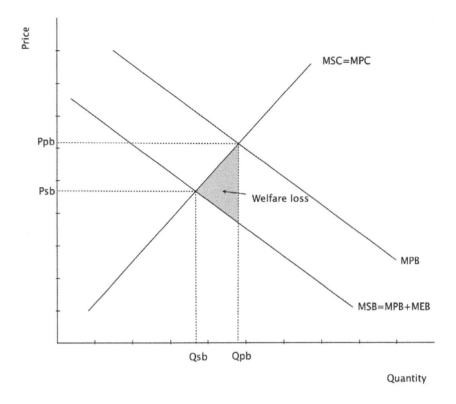

There are several policy options open to governments looking to cure the problems of negative externalities.

- **Taxation** (see diagrams on pages 23-4)

The benefit of a tax is that it simply shifts the supply curve upwards, increasing MPC to MSC. Good examples of this approach are environmental taxes: taxes on fuel, for example, landfill taxes, and, more recently, carbon taxes. Here, the polluter pays.

There are several problems with taxing negative externalities.

- **Setting a tax to represent MEC.** It is very difficult to calculate accurately a monetary value of the spillover effects of a negative externality.
- **Goods with a price inelastic demand curve.** Here, producers can pass most of the tax burden onto consumers, and so output/consumption will not radically be reduced.
- **The regressive nature of some taxation.** Income inequality may be widened.
- **International competitiveness.** If a country takes a unilateral action to tax negative externalities, it may make its exports less competitive as prices rise.
- **Optimal tax rates.** High taxes might not reduce consumption at all, but create black markets and other illegal activities.

- **Tradable Permits**

Tradable permits are used to limit the negative activities of firms. These can vary from the emission of polluting gases to the overfishing of the North Sea. The optimal level of pollution or

> Good candidates will be able to analyse and evaluate the various policy options available to cure market failures. They will realise that curing market failures is often not a clear-cut issue, and nearly all cures have both benefits and costs.

production is set by a government or regulatory body, and this total is then divided into individual firm permits to pollute or produce. Firms are able both to buy and sell these permits. In the case of pollution, firms have an obvious incentive to be environmentally efficient so they can sell their permits to other firms (a very profitable activity). In the case of production permits, firms are allowed to maintain their income while they are not producing (for example a North Sea trawler might be out of action through repairs, but could still rent out their permits to other firms). Also, efficient producers can buy quotas from less efficient firms to increase their output.

These tradable permits are presently one of the front-line responses to market failure.

- **Regulation**

Governments can intervene directly with measures such as quotas to set the optimal level of production/consumption. Most firms today have to comply with minimum environmental requirements. For example, building regulations in the UK stipulate minimum insulation requirements for all new buildings.

There are several problems with regulation:

- **Setting a limit.** It is very easy to over- or underestimate a limit that coincides with a socially efficient outcome.
- **Costs of regulation.** All forms of regulations are costly to administer and enforce.
- **Benefits greater than costs.** Some firms will still not reduce pollution if the benefits from pollution are greater than the costs of doing so (fines).

- **Extending property rights**

Property rights are the legal right to own or to do something. If individuals have the legal right to clean air, for example, and this right is easily and effectively enforced through the courts, then polluting activities can be stopped, and/or financial recompense is available.

This approach is only effective in societies where property rights are easily enforced. This is often not the case in many economically less developed economies and also many of the previously centrally-planned economies.

- **International co-operation**

The 1997 United Nations pact signed at Kyoto required the major industrialised nations to make meaningful reductions in greenhouse gas emissions. The EU's target was to cut 1990 emission levels by 8% before 2010. In 2004 a report stated that only two countries (UK and Sweden) out of the then 15 would be able to meet these targets. Of course, the USA still refuses to sign up to the treaty and this is a major blow to any international agreement to cut emissions. International agreements are beset by political problems with the process of negotiation often taking some time. Policing of agreements is very difficult and there are great incentives to 'cheat'. In October 2004 Russia agreed to ratify the Kyoto agreement. Now 30 countries are committed to legally binding reductions in greenhouse gasses (5% on 1990 levels).

Positive externalities

A good example of a positive externality is the environmentally beneficial effects of bee-keeping. Bees pollinate plants and increase crop yields. They are best illustrated as positive externalities from consumption. *Here, the market fails to measure the true benefits of consumption to society.* In a free market the demand curve measures the **marginal private benefit** (MPB), but it fails to measure the **marginal external benefit** (MEB). The true benefit to society, the **marginal social benefit** (MSB) is equal to MPB + MEB. The shaded area below is lost welfare due to underconsumption:

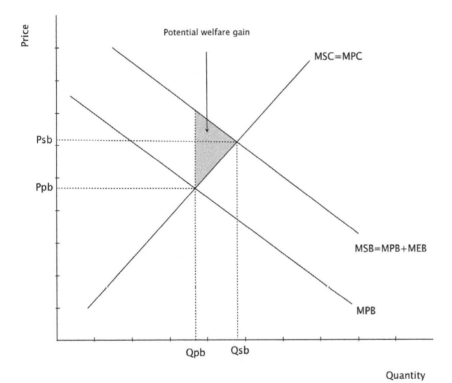

The free market equilibrium (where demand = supply, or marginal social cost MSC = MPB) results in both underproduction and underconsumption of the good or service. In the diagram above, this is output level Qpb. If the market were to take into account the true benefits of consumption, as shown by the MSB curve, then output/consumption would be at Qsb (socially optimal level). Here the free market has failed to allocate resources efficiently, and has underproduced/ consumed goods with positive spillover effects.

The shaded area below represents the welfare loss to society created by this underconsumption. Here, each good has a MSB that is greater than its MSC. In this example, we have assumed that there is no negative externality in production, and therefore marginal private costs are equal to marginal social costs.

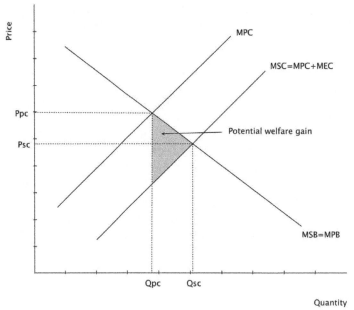

There are several policy options open to governments looking to increase the consumption of goods with positive externalities.

- **Subsidies**

Subsidies aim to reduce the marginal private costs (MPC) of production until the equilibrium level of output is reached (QSB). As with taxes in the case of negative externalities, the problem here is one of information. It is very hard to gain accurate estimates of costs, benefits and the external effects associated with positive externalities. If demand is price inelastic, then a subsidy will only result in a small increase in consumption.

- **Free Provision**

In many countries both education and most healthcare services are provided free of charge at the point of consumption.

- **Information**

One of the best ways of increasing the consumption of goods with positive externalities is to educate and inform people of the benefits, and so encourage people to make informed consumption choices.

Public Goods

Here the market fails because the key features of **public goods** are ***non-excludability*** and ***non-rivalry*** in consumption.

> **Non-excludability** means that *even if you have paid for a good you cannot confine its use to yourself.*
> **Non-rivalry** means that *the consumption of a good does not reduce its availability to others.*

Good examples of public goods are national defence and street-lighting.

In a free market, public goods would not be provided because of the two above features, and because individuals could **free-ride** on others' consumption.

Merit and Demerit Goods

Here the market fails because consumers make choices which society defines as wrong. In the case of **merit goods**, *consumers consume too few goods and services that are seen as being good for them* (like education, art galleries). In the case of **demerit goods**, *consumers consume too many goods and services that are seen as being bad for them* (alcohol and cigarettes, for example). Merit goods can also (but not always) have positive externalities. Demerit goods can also (but not always) have negative externalities.

> It is important that you do not automatically assume that merit goods are goods with positive externalities and vice versa, and that demerit goods are goods with negative externalities and vice versa. This is an area in which candidates often muddle their definitions.

If merit and demerit goods do have externalities, then the cures mentioned above can be used. But education and information are very valid approaches, as consumer choices are at the heart of the failure of the market mechanism.

Monopoly Power

A detailed diagrammatic analysis of market power is undertaken in the Market Structures section of this Revision Guide.

Here the market fails because **monopolies** (*single sellers, or firms with 100% market share*) erect **barriers to entry**, preventing competition. These barriers enable them to develop **market power** (*the ability to increase prices*). Monopolies will tend to result in both higher prices and lower output, and a decrease in **economic efficiency** (with prices greater than market cost and output not produced at minimum average cost), although, as we shall see later on, this might not necessarily always be the case.

> Along with externalities, this is the key area of market failure on which exams focus. You should be prepared to answer both short answer and essay questions on monopolies and the comparison of monopoly with other market forms, especially perfect competition. Whilst the diagrammatic analysis is both detailed and complex, it is a very well-structured part of the syllabus. With some careful planning, therefore, you should be able to produce well-directed written answers to examination questions.

There are a wide variety of **cures for market power** open to government:

- **Banning**

The formation of monopolies can be banned and existing monopolies split up. This is the approach taken by the Sherman Act in America.

- **Investigation and Regulation**

Most countries have organisations that investigate concentrating markets (in the UK this is the Competition Commission in combination with the Office of Fair Trading). These organisations make decisions about whether or not mergers/takeovers/ monopolies are in the public interest. They also investigate trading practices. Recent examples include the concentration of UK supermarkets, concern over the actions of Microsoft in America, and the EU competition ruling on the production of vitamin supplements. The powers that individual regulatory organisations have vary widely from country to country (from fines to prison sentences).

- **Regulation of Privatised Industries**

Most economies have privatised some or many of their previous nationalised industries in recent decades. Because these risk becoming private monopolies, they tend to be regulated in terms of price and quality of service provision, alongside measures to reduce barriers to entry and therefore encourage competition. This has been especially true in the UK.

- **Laissez-faire**

Some economists suggest that the problems created by monopolies are best cured by the actions of a free market.

Common Access Resources and Sustainability

Common Access Resources are *resources that are available to everyone without payment, do not have a price, and are not owned by anyone.* Good examples are clean air, fish in the sea, and biodiversity. It is not possible to exclude anyone from using these resources (they are non-excludable), however, their use reduces their availability to others (they are rivalrous). As these resources have no price, they are overused, resulting in serious environmental degradation and depletion.

Sustainability happens when *resources are used today in such a way that does not compromise their use by future generations.* Here we have a conflict between the economic goal of growth and the environmental goal of sustainability. The concept of negative externalities can be used here to illustrate how economic activity threatens sustainability. Government responses to sustainability can be linked into government responses to negative externalities (legislation, carbon taxes, cap and trade schemes).

The major problem is the global nature of sustainability. 'Common access' means 'world-wide access', so effective response requires international co-operation. A good example of this is the European Union Emissions Trading System (a carbon dioxide permit scheme with trading in a carbon market).

Asymmetric Information

Sometimes, *buyers and sellers do not have equal information about the market in which the economic transaction is taking place.* Used car sellers and homeowners have more information than potential buyers. If consumers are concerned about possible dangers from consumption, then they will underconsume. If consumers are unaware of possible dangers, then they will overconsume. Both of these scenarios result in a misallocation of resources.

Governments can respond through legislation, regulation and the provision of information. A major problem occurs when a risk-taking party does not face the full costs of their risks. This type of asymmetric information and lack of moral hazard has been seen as one of the major causes of the financial crisis that begun in 2008.

MICROECONOMICS SAMPLE QUESTIONS

Microeconomics is examined in Paper 1 (extended response/ essay) Section A.

1. (a) Explain the importance of cross elasticity of demand and price elasticity of demand for firms when making decisions. (10 marks)

   (b) Studies have shown that the demand for petrol tends to be highly price inelastic. Evaluate a policy of substantially raising taxes on petrol as a method of reducing its consumption. (15 marks)

2. (a) Using diagrams, explain the difference between a perfectly competitive firm, in terms of profits, in the short-run and the long-run. (10 marks)

   (b) Evaluate the view that perfect competition is a more desirable market structure than monopoly. (15 marks)

Model markschemes to these questions are on pages 126-40.

SECTION 2: MACROECONOMICS

MEASURING NATIONAL INCOME

> You need to know how to calculate various measures of national income for the data response paper, but apart from that you should not concern yourself too much with them.

National income = national output = national expenditure

Income method = payments to factors of production

Output method = the value of final output produced by various industrial sectors

Expenditure method = **GDP** = C + I + G + (X-M)
- C = consumption
- I = investment
- G = government spending
- X = exports
- M = imports.

GDP is the total value of output produced in an economy in a given time period.

GNI = GDP + net property income from abroad

NNI = GNI – depreciation (capital consumption)

Factor cost = market prices – indirect taxes + subsidies

Real GDP/GNI = nominal GDP/GNI – inflation

GDP/GNI **per capita** = GDP/GNI / population

Green GDP = GDP – environmental costs of production

There are problems with GDP as a measure of national income. GDP itself does not take into account the negative spillover effects of economic activity or the degradation of natural resources. However, it also underestimates national income by failing to measure black market activity, unpaid work carried out by volunteers or housework and care for family members, and does not take into account of improvements in the quality of output.

Numerical application:
Calculate GDP, GNP/ GNI
Real GDP and base year prices

Circular Flow of Income

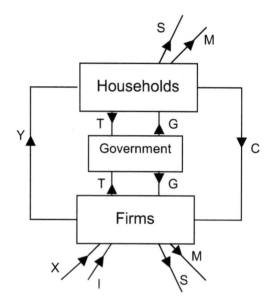

Income flowing into the flow is known as **injections** (J), and income flowing out of the flow is known as **withdrawals** (W).

$$J = G + I + X$$
$$W = T + S + M$$

Equilibrium level of national income exists when planned J = planned W. This equilibrium level of income might not necessarily coincide with the full employment level of national income. The total level of income in the circular flow at any given time period is equal to national income.

Business Cycle Model

The business/trade cycle shows a pattern of growth (around a trend rate of growth) of boom, recession, trough and recovery measured by changes in real GDP, as shown in the diagram below.

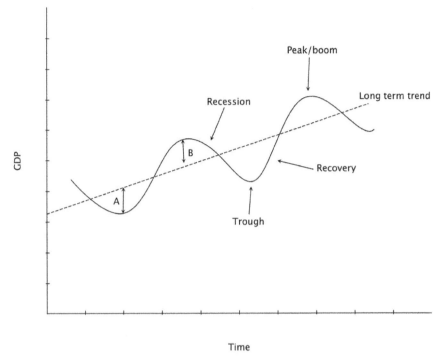

Recession (Two consecutive quarters of negative GDP growth)
- Rising unemployment
- Falling consumption
- Falling investment
- Increasing government spending and falling tax revenue
- Business failures

Recovery (a period of economic growth post-recession)
- Falling unemployment
- Increasing consumption
- Increasing investment
- Rising inflation

Boom (an extended period of above-trend growth)
- Accelerating inflation
- Shortages of scarce factors (skilled labour)
- Rapidly rising property and equity values

Trough (lowest level of GDP in the cycle)
- Widespread long-term unemployment

Fluctuations in growth are shown in fluctuations in actual output. The long-term trend rate of growth shows the rate of growth that an economy can sustain over time (potential growth). The difference between actual and potential growth is the **output gap**. At A there is a negative output gap and at B there is a positive output gap.

A decrease in GDP (where the economy actually shrinks) is different from a decrease in GDP growth (where the economy continues to grow, but at a slower rate).

MACROECONOMIC MODELS

Aggregate Demand and Supply Analysis

AD and AS analysis is the main system for analysing macro-economic problems and policies. Once mastered, it is a very flexible tool which is easily brought into any macro-economic situation. You should be able to manipulate AD/AS diagrams accurately to explain any macroeconomic situation.

Equilibrium level of national income is where *aggregate demand (AD) is equal to aggregate supply (AS)*.

- **Aggregate Demand**

AD = Consumption (C) + Investment (I) + Government Expenditure (G) + (Exports (X) – Imports (M)).

AD is the *total demand for an economy's goods and services*.

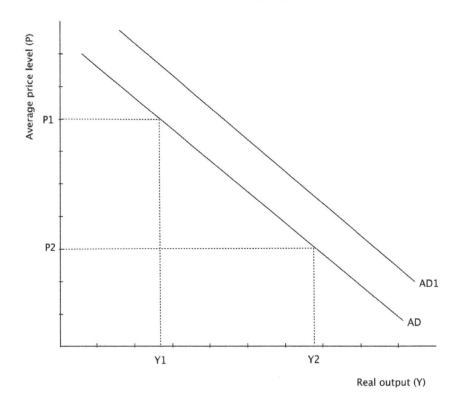

AD is downward-sloping because as prices rise, the demand for an economy's goods and services will be less. Goods will be less competitive in international markets and real income is less.

AD will shift if any of C + I + G + (X – M) change.

Factors that influence **consumption**:
- Consumer confidence
- Interest rates
- Wealth
- Income taxes
- Debt

Factors that influence **investment**:
- Interest rates
- Taxes on profits and investment

- Business confidence
- Corporate debt

Factors that influence **government spending**:
- Political and economic priorities

Factors that influence **net exports**:
- Exchange rates
- Protectionism
- Income levels of trading partners

Important Factors that shift the AD curve are:

Fiscal policy. An increase in government spending will increase AD, and a decrease in government spending will decrease AD. A decrease in taxation will increase AD, as it will increase disposable income and thus C. An increase in taxation will decrease AD as it will decrease disposable income and thus C. Thus, a budget deficit (G > T) will increase AD and a budget surplus (G < T) will decrease AD. Expansionary fiscal policy (increasing AD) can thus be used to 'close' a deflationary gap and deflationary fiscal policy (decreasing AD) can be used to 'close' an inflationary gap.

Monetary policy. An increase in the rate of interest will decrease AD by increasing saving and so reducing consumption, by decreasing investment, and by strengthening the exchange rate and so reducing exports. A decrease in the rate of interest would have the opposite effect. An increase in the money supply may be used to increase AD.

Exchange Rates. An increase in the value of an economy's currency will, other things being equal, make an economy's exports less competitive and imports more competitive and so reduce AD. The opposite is also the case.

Of course, **ceteris paribus** applies to all these factors.

> Diagrams to illustrate these demand-side policies can be found where this guide discusses Macro Equilibrium and the different approaches taken by Keynesian and Monetarist/Neo-Classical Economists. You should be able to draw AD/AS diagrams that illustrate the impacts of expansionary fiscal and monetary policies as well, enabling you to discuss the importance of the shape of the AS curves when analysing and evaluating policy.

- **Aggregate Supply**
AS represents *the total value of goods and services that an economy can produce in a given time period.*

> There is a lot of controversy over the shape of the AS curve. The shape affects the final outcome of any shift in the AD curve. The implication of macro policies and the potential solutions to macro problems all depend upon one's view of the shape of the AS curve. There is, however, agreement over the AS curve being vertical when an economy reaches full employment. The disagreement lies in whether an economy is always at full employment or not. Keynesians believe that an economy may not necessarily be in equilibrium at full employment.

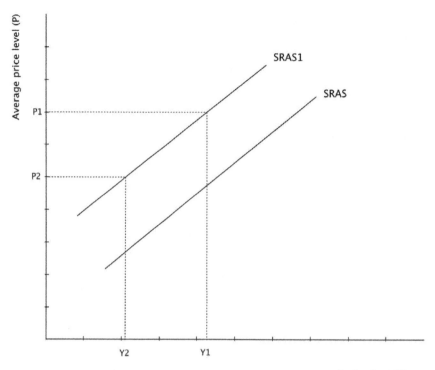

In the short run AS slopes upwards because, as prices rise, firms find it profitable to increase their output, and new firms will start producing.

Factors that shift **SRAS**:
- Changes to raw material and component costs
- Business taxes and subsidies
- Changes to labour costs
- Supply-side shocks

In the long run, AS is vertical as the economy is at full capacity. Output cannot therefore be increased in responses to increases in aggregate demand.

Factors that shift **LRAS**:
- Changes to the stock of productive resources
- Changes to productivity/efficiency
- Changes to technology
- Institutional changes

These factors lead to changes in the quantity and/or quality of factors of production.

- **Alternative views of LRAS**
Keynsian
Different levels of spare capacity in an economy give the aggregate supply curve three distinct sections:

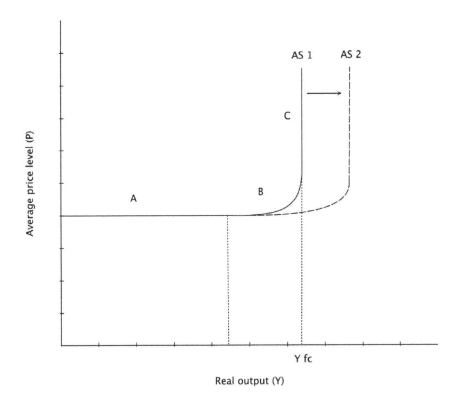

Real output (Y)

In section 'A' above, there is plenty of spare capacity in the economy and so output can be increased without increasing costs. In section 'B' shortages of some factors exist and so increases in output will cause prices to rise as the cost of hiring these scarce factors increases. In section 'C' the economy is at full employment (in the long run and at full capacity) and so any attempt to increase output will be purely inflationary.

An improvement in the quantity and/or quality of factors of production will shift the long run aggregate supply section of the Keynesian AS curve to the right (AS1 to AS2).

Monetarlst/ New Classical
In the following graph, LRAS is vertical at the full employment level of output (full capacity and potential output). As potential output is based on factors (their quantity and quality), the price level does not affect LRAS. Employment is determined in factor markets and this determines the total level of output in an economy.

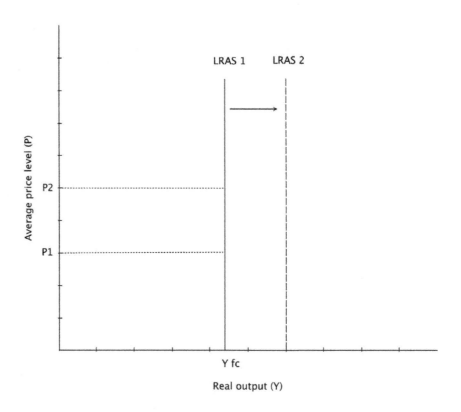

- **Equilibrium**

Macroeconomic equilibrium is where AD = AS:

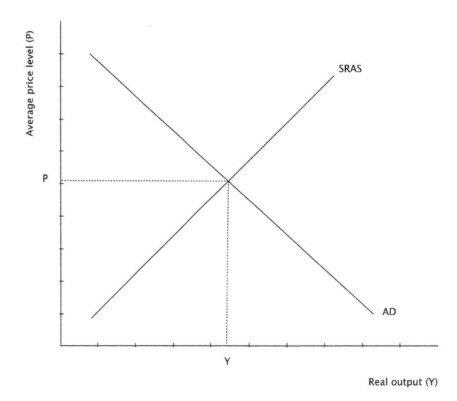

Here, short run equilibrium is where AD=SRAS.

In the Keynesian model, the economy is at equilibrium where AD=AS (actual output) at any level of output. If equilibrium is below full employment (actual < potential output) then there is a deflationary (recessionary) gap (Y1 and Y2 < Yfc in the diagram below). This 'gap 'is also known as a negative output gap. Here growth need not be inflationary, as there is spare capacity in the economy.

You should be careful not to get too hung up on the differences between Keynesians and Monetarists unless the questions ask you clearly to distinguish between these two schools of thought. You need to be able to use AD and AS analysis effectively to analyse and evaluate economic issues, and so you should use an AS curve that allows for both analysis of the short and the long run. I would use the diagrams on the left and right to do this.

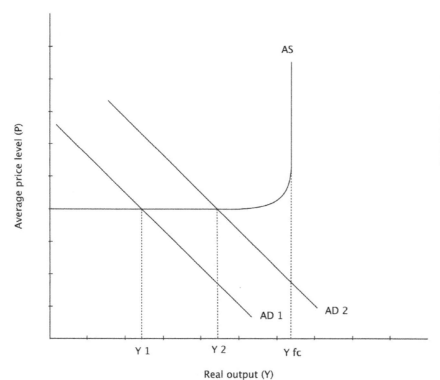

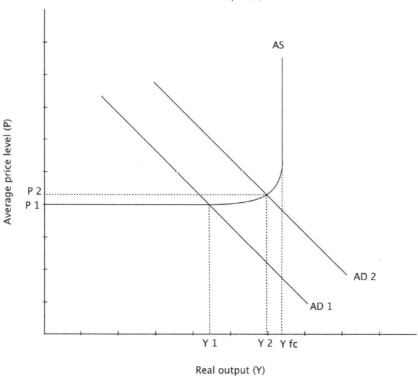

At equilibrium levels of output below full capacity (Yfc), Keynesian economists would suggest that demand side policies should be used to increase output, as shown above.

Any increase in AD at full capacity (Yfc) will be purely inflationary (inflationary gap where actual > potential), as there is no spare capacity in the economy:

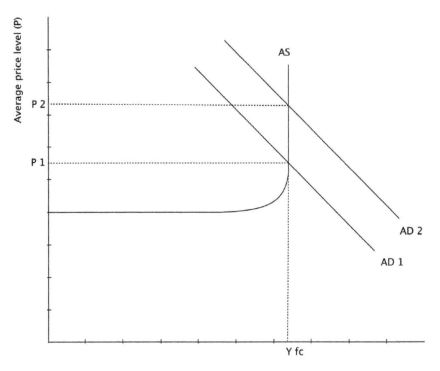

Monetarists and New Classical economists believe that an economy is always at full employment, and therefore the AS curve is vertical.

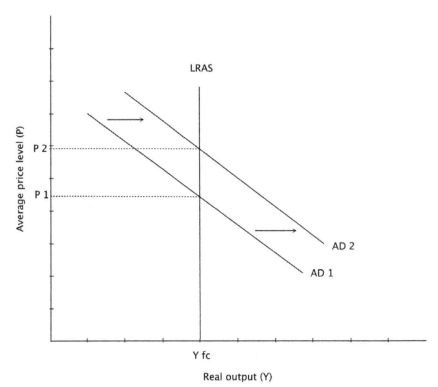

As you can see in the diagram above, any increase in AD will be purely inflationary in the long run.

At full employment, the only way to increase national income and reduce unemployment without causing inflation is to use supply-side policies to move the LRAS curve outwards to the right (LRAS 1 to LRAS2):

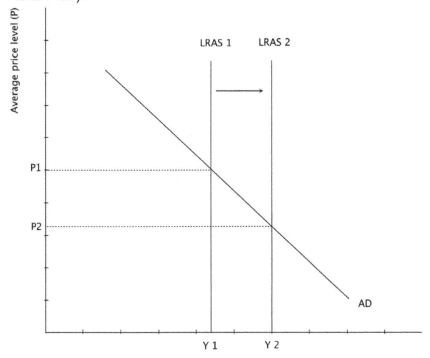

Increasing AD at full employment reduces unemployment in the short run, but creates an inflationary gap. Output can only be increased by paying existing factors of production more (overtime), so rising costs of production will shift SRAS to SRAS*, returning output to the full employment level, but at a higher price level (P*):

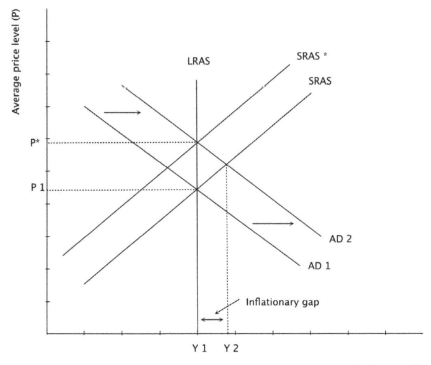

With falling AD the opposite happens via a deflationary gap (actual output is less than potential output):

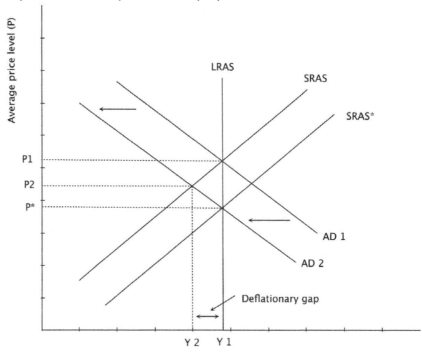

In order to increase output in the long run, policy should aim to increase LRAS (LRAS1 to LRAS2) using supply-side policies.

Macroeconomic policy is in effect a balance between demand-side and supply-side policies. AD can be allowed or encouraged to increase as long as there is room on the supply side for it to do so. Most developed economies can only sustain a 2-3% growth rate of national income without causing inflation to accelerate.

Governments need to use demand-side policies (fiscal and monetary policies) to make sure that AD does not grow out of control (unsustainably), whilst using supply-side policies to encourage the growth of productive potential to make sure that economic growth is sustainable at low levels of inflation. Of course many developing economies can sustain much higher growth rates. Currently China is 'targeting' a 7% growth rate with a 4% inflation target.

Students frequently find this a very confusing area. Both schools of thought seem to have persuasive arguments to account for the way in which the economic world works. Good economics is about differing opinions! The extremist proponents of these two schools of thought will carry on arguing well into the future.

The Keynesian/Monetarist Debate

Keynesians believe that:
- Markets are slow to adjust
- An economy can be in equilibrium below full employment
- Governments should and can effectively intervene to stabilise an economy
- Fiscal is more effective than monetary policy

Monetarists believe that:
- Markets work
- Economies tend towards full employment
- Inflation is caused by excessive money supply growth
- Governments should intervene really only to control inflation by controlling money supply growth

The Multiplier

The **multiplier effect** *is the proportion by which an initial increase in injections, or reduction in withdrawals, causes a greater final increase in the level of national income.*

The size of the multiplier depends upon the marginal propensities to consume (MPC) and withdrawal (MPW = MPS + MPT + MPM). The greater the MPC (the less the MPW), the greater the multiplier will be, as all income is either consumed or withdrawn (Y = C + W). This is because a greater proportion of an increase in income will be spent with domestic firms. Household saving and consumption plans are difficult to predict, and so the value of the multiplier is hard to predict and it may change over time.

Numerical application:
Calculate MPC and MPW (MPS + MPT + MPM) from the data
Calculate the value of the multiplier:

$$\frac{1}{(1-MPC)}$$

$$\frac{1}{(MPW)}$$

Calculate effect on GDP of a change in an injection
Determine the level of G or I needed to generate a given change in GDP

DEMAND-SIDE AND SUPPLY-SIDE POLICIES

Demand-side Policies

- **Fiscal Policy**

Fiscal policy is *the use of government spending (current, capital and transfer payments) and taxation (direct and indirect) to influence AD, raise revenue, redistribute income and influence consumption patterns.* A government's **fiscal stance** is how expansionary or contractionary their budget is. The way in which government spending and taxation influences AD has already been mentioned above, but there can be problems with fiscal policy.

The government budget:
Budget **deficit** is when total expenditure > total tax revenue (in a particular year).
Budget **surplus** is when total expenditure < total tax revenue (in a particular year).

National debt is *the accumulation of all the past years' deficits.* A budget deficit will increase the size of the national debt. A budget surplus will reduce the size of the national debt.

Government expenditure:
- Current: spending on factor payments and goods
- Capital: investment spending and spending on assets
- Transfer payments: a payment from the government to an individual (eg. unemployed or pensioner) where no output is generated. It is a means of redistribution of income

Government revenue:
- Direct taxes: taxes on income (wages/salaries, interest, dividends, rent and profit)
- Indirect taxes: taxes on expenditure (paid indirectly by firms supplying goods and services)
- Sale of goods, services and the privatisation of nationalised industries

Automatic (built-in) stabilizers:
In most economies there is an element of automatic fiscal policy creating some stability in GDP. As GDP grows, government spending decreases (falling benefit payments) and taxation increases (progressive taxes). As output and GDP fall government spending increases and taxation falls. This 'built-in' process seeks to help stabilize short-term fluctuations in GDP.

Fiscal Policy strengths/weaknesses:
Strengths:
- Targetable
- Direct impact on AD
- Role in recession

Weaknesses:
- Time lags
- Political influence
- Inflexible
- Budget deficits can lead to increases in interest rates (to encourage bond sales) and taxation in the future
- Crowding-out is when government bond sales result in the public sector needing to compete with the private sector for funds. They will have to offer higher rates of interest in order to sell bonds, and the availability of funds in the loanable fund market will decrease. Thus the private sector will be forced to offer high interest rates as well, discouraging investment and

spending. Some economists argue that this will only happen when an economy is at full capacity

Because of the limitations of fiscal policy, most governments focus their demand-side policies around monetary policy and the rate of interest in particular. Fiscal policy is now often used to improve the supply-side of an economy, for example by cutting direct taxes and benefits.

Fiscal policy and potential output (LRAS):
Fiscal policy can be, and is increasingly, used to increase potential output and thus long-run economic growth. Creating incentives via the tax system for firms to invest and individuals to work, creating an environment that is favourable for business and employment and actual government spending on infrastructure are all examples of fiscal policies that target potential output.

• Monetary Policy
Monetary policy is *the use of the rate of interest predominantly to influence AD (the money supply control and targeting the exchange rate can also be used).*

Equilibrium interest rates are determined in the money market and central banks can influence interest rates by either increasing/decreasing the money supply or changing interest rates and then changing the money supply to support this decision.

In the graph below, the interest rate is determined by the demand (D m) for and supply (S m1 and S m2) of money. Here an increase in the money supply (S m1 to S m2) results in a fall in the rate of interest:

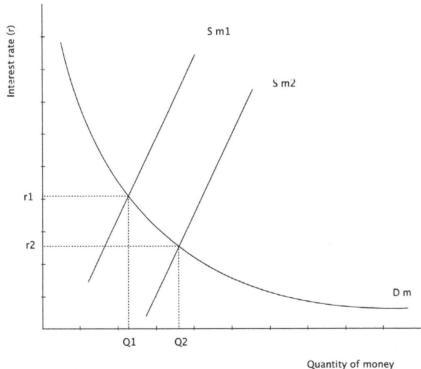

The role of the central bank:

- Banker to the government
- Regulates the commercial banking system
- Manages government's borrowing by issuing bonds to finance budget deficit
- Sets interest rates to achieve macro targets (eg. inflation targeting in the Eurozone and the UK)
- Manages the supply of money through nominal interest rates, the issue of notes and, more recently, quantitative easing
- Manages gold and foreign currency reserves (the exchange rate)

Inflation targeting:
As a response to the failure of discretionary macroeconomic policies, many countries have turned to inflation targeting as their 'core' macroeconomic policy. Here, monetary policy focuses on the rate of inflation rather than a broad set of frequently-conflicting macro goals. Interest rates (and sometimes the money supply) are used to achieve a target that is either symmetrical (Canada 2% +/- 1%) or asymmetrical (Eurozone <2%). Once the target has been achieved, it is then 'simply' a matter of using interest rates to maintain the target level.

During the first few years of the 21st century, in most developed economies, economic growth did not seem to generate inflation as it had done so in the past, and inflation targets were achieved with relative ease. When inflation did appear it was mainly generated by rising commodity prices, resulting from rapid growth in countries such as India and China. Inflation was seen to be have been cost-driven and so seen as 'temporal' so a simple interest rate response (increasing rates) would have reduced AD, causing slow growth/a recession rather than hitting the 'cost-push' causes of inflation. Supply-side shocks continued to cause inflationary 'spikes' in 2008 and 2011, despite a period of recession and slow growth for the world economy, and therefore, since then, many central banks kept their bank rates low and took a more 'flexible' approach to inflation targeting.

Monetary Policy strengths/weaknesses:
Strengths
- Independence of central banks removes political influence
- Incremental changes are possible
- Relative speed of change

Weaknesses

- Investment can be interest-inelastic
- Time lags
- One policy fits all (blunt instrument)
- Ineffective against cost-push inflation
- Low consumer/investor confidence in deep recession mean that consumers and firms fail to respond to low borrowing rates and may pay back debts instead of borrowing

Most developed economies now actively use the rate of interest to influence AD. Independent central banks dominate rate of interest decision-making. They are able to respond instantly to changing economic circumstances, whereas fiscal policy often has to wait for the democratic wheels to turn.

Supply-side Policies

Supply-side policies aim to increase an economy's productive potential by changing the quantity and/or quality of resources in the economy, as shown in the following two diagrams:

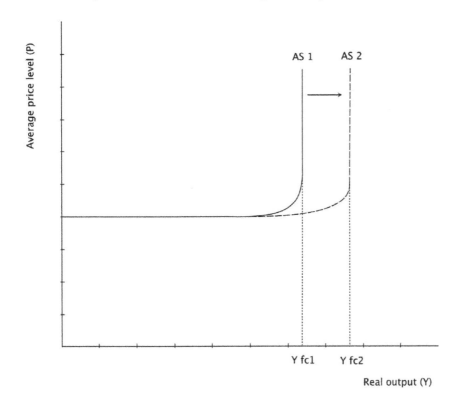

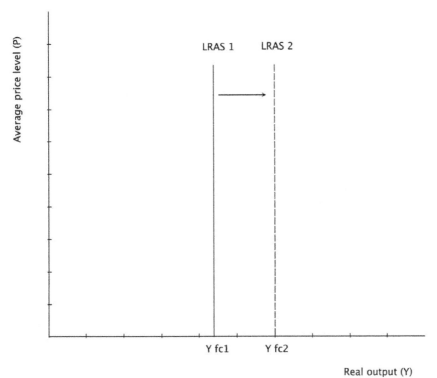

Policies can either be market-based or interventionist.

Interventionist-based:
- Investment in human capital
- Investment in new technology
- Investment in infrastructure
- Industrial policy

Here the individual needs of countries may differ significantly and the needs of ELDCs differ considerably from developed economies. There may well be negative effects on a government's budget, and time lags can be substantial.

Market-based:
- Deregulation, privatisation and encouraging competition
- Labour market reforms
- Incentives to work and invest (firms)

These policies can result in increased monopoly power for firms and reduced incomes/job protection and health and safety measures for workers. They will also redistribute income and the impact of incentives is not clear as individuals respond in different ways to the same policies.

UNEMPLOYMENT AND INFLATION

Essays ask easy factual questions about the types, causes and cures of both unemployment and inflation.

Unemployment

The **Unemployed** *are the people who are registered as willing, able and available for work at the market-clearing wage, but who are unable to find work.*

The **Unemployment Rate** *is the number of people unemployed as a percentage of the labour force.*

Underemployment *is when workers who want full-time jobs are only able to find part-time employment. Low wages and output per worker are reflections of work with low rates of productivity.*

Hidden Unemployment *is the part of the working population excluded from any measure of unemployment because of the definition of unemployment used.*

One of the major problems with any measure of unemployment is that it is an aggregated and average measure that takes no account of regional, gender, age and ethnic variations and disparities.

The **costs of unemployment** are:
- Loss of output

- Waste of productive potential
- Loss of skills
- Government finances (loss of tax revenue, increased benefit spending)
- Social problems
- Loss of consumer spending
- Increased income disparity

The **types (causes) of unemployment** are:
- Cyclical (Demand Deficient)
- Frictional
- Seasonal
- Structural

- **Equilibrium unemployment**

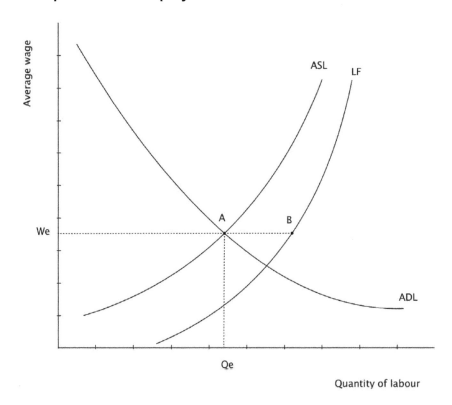

Here, A to B is the equilibrium level of unemployment (natural level of unemployment). The main causes of this type of unemployment are frictional, seasonal and structural. ASL is the aggregate supply of labour and LF is the labour force. At We the quantity of labour willing and able to work at We is less than the labour force. Jobs are available, however, A to B workers are not willing or able to work at the market-clearing wage.

Solutions to **frictional (search)** unemployment include incentivising unemployed workers to take job opportunities (eg. reducing benefit levels) or providing information about available vacancies. Similar solutions can also be applied to **seasonal** unemployment.

Solutions to **structural** unemployment (a mismatch between skills and opportunities caused by technological change, a fall in demand for a particular job/skill and changes in consumers tastes) focus on supply-side policies to increase the mobility (in terms of skill, occupation and geography) of labour. Education, training (apprenticeships) and relocation incentives all target structural causes of unemployment.

- **Disequilibrium unemployment**

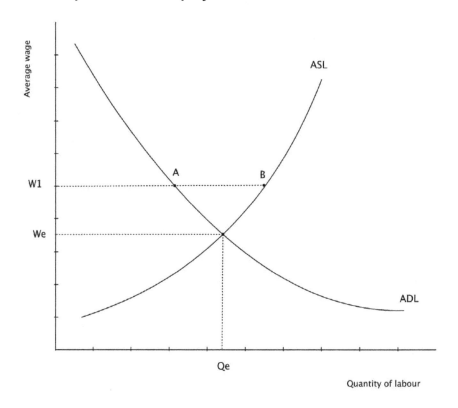

Here, with W1 above We, A to B represents unemployment as 'sticky' wages stop the wage rate falling to We (equilibrium wage rate). A good example of this is unemployment caused by trade unions and minimum wages (real wage/classical unemployment).

Demand deficient unemployment is caused by recessions. As shown in the following graph, as aggregate demand falls (AD1 to AD2), firms reduce employment as the demand for their output falls:

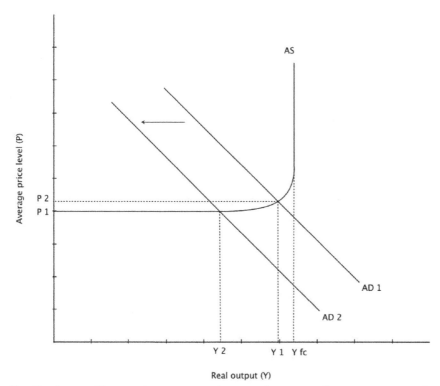

Cyclical or Keynesian unemployment sees the economy in equilibrium below the full employment level of income (Yfc), and so policy here would aim to increase AD by the use of fiscal and/or monetary policies.

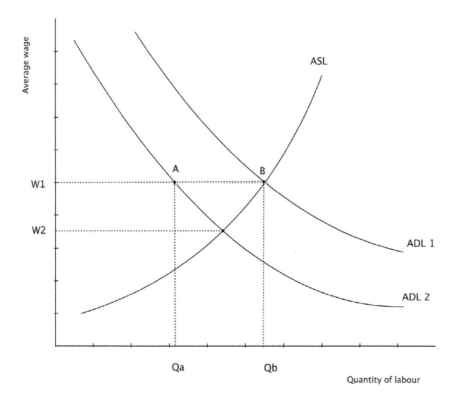

Here the demand for labour falls from ADL 1 to ADL 2, and with wages reluctant to fall, disequilibrium unemployment exists from A to B.

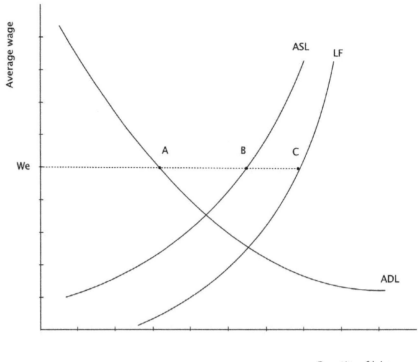

Quantity of labour

Of course, several causes of unemployment may 'coexist' in an economy at any given time period. In the diagram above, A to B is disequilibrium unemployment and B to C is equilibrium unemployment, and so different strategies are needed to cure the overall problem.

• **The Natural Rate of Unemployment**
The **natural rate**, also known as the **equilibrium rate**, *is any unemployment that exists when the aggregate demand for labour equals the aggregate supply of labour.* **Supply-side policies** should be used as a cure. The natural rate exists at the full employment level of income (where there is no demand deficient unemployment), and this is where the AS curve is vertical. This again emphasises the need for supply-side policies.

Numerical application:
Calculate unemployment rate from data

Inflation

Inflation is *a constant rise in prices over a given time period.* There are problems with the measurement of inflation. Should mortgage payments and indirect taxes be included? Is a weighted basket system (Consumer Price Index) fully representative of all people's costs of living, and does it take into account the change in quality of goods and services produced?

Disinflation is *a fall in the rate of inflation.*

Core/underlying inflation *excludes the impacts of volatile prices* (oil and food are good current examples).

Producer price index (PPI) *measures inflation using a 'basket' factors that are used in the production process (eg. capital, raw materials and energy prices).* This measure gives us an indication of the extent to which SRAS might be affected by price changes.

- **The consequences of inflation:**
- Redistribution of income (savers versus borrowers, weak versus strong bargainers in the labour market, fixed incomes)
- Devaluation of money/loss of purchasing power
- Reduction of investment
- Reduction of international competitiveness
- A potential for a wage-price spiral if inflation runs out of control
- Shoe-leather and menu costs

Many of the costs of inflation depend upon whether inflation is anticipated or unanticipated. Volatile inflation makes it difficult for businesses and individuals to plan and predict inflation in the short to medium term. Volatility results in businesses and individuals taking steps to protect their interests. The overall impact of inflation is therefore a reduction in economic growth combined with an increase in unemployment.

- **The types (causes) of inflation:**

Cost-push inflation can be caused by:
- Rising raw material costs
- Rising labour costs
- Increased indirect taxation
- Currency depreciation

Cost-push inflation is shown in the diagram below by a decrease in SRAS resulting in an increase in the average price level from P_1 to P_2.

Macro policies are rather ineffective at attempting to cure cost-push inflation in the short run, as a demand-side focus is not appropriate and supply-side policies are only really effective in the long run.

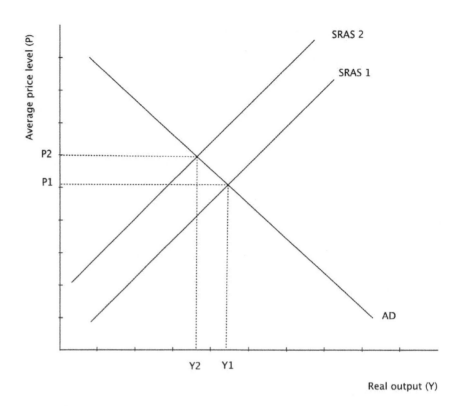

Demand-pull inflation can be caused by:
- Reduced taxation
- Increased government spending
- Reduced interest rates
- Rising consumer confidence stimulated by rising asset prices
- Economic growth in other countries
- Depreciation of a country's exchange rate

Demand-pull inflation is shown in the diagram below by an increase in AD when near or at full employment, resulting in an increase in price level from P_1 P2 and P_3.

Any increase in a component of AD can cause demand–pull inflation.

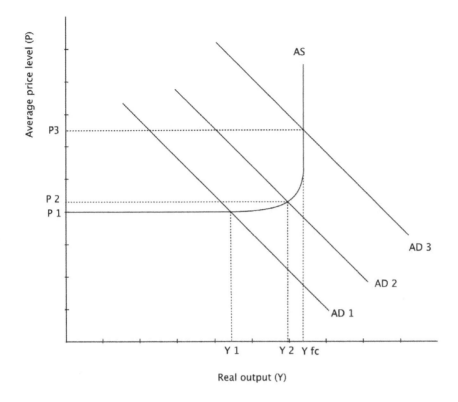

Real output (Y)

As output nears full employment (Yfc), factors of production become scarcer and competition for limited output drives up prices.

Here, cures for inflation should focus on reducing the rate of growth of aggregate demand or, in extreme circumstances, actually reducing aggregate demand and national income.

- **The cures for inflation:**

Demand side:
- Monetary policy (an increase in interest rates)
- Fiscal policy (reducing government spending and/or increasing direct taxation)

Supply side:
- Policies to increase the total supply of goods and services by an economy

> It is important that fiscal and monetary policies work in tandem. There is no point in tightening monetary policy if it is contradicted by a slackening of fiscal policy.

The control of inflation is a balancing act between AD and AS. Governments or independent central banks need to keep control of the rate of growth of AD whilst policies are needed to continually expand an economy's productive capacity. Increased output produced at lower cost gives an economy room to grow without causing rising inflation.

Deflation *is a constant fall in prices over a given time period.*

Demand-side deflation is a dangerous type of deflation and is caused by a fall in AD linked to a time of recession (AD1 to AD2, in the diagram below). As a recession extends in time employment falls and there is downward pressure on prices.

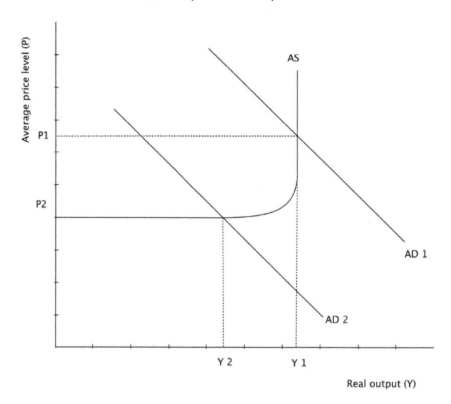

With rising unemployment, falling investment, rising saving and falling consumption, unchecked deflation can result in delayed consumption and further deflation. It is crucial that this type of deflation is checked by demand-side policies to increase AD.

Supply-side deflation from lower commodity and oil prices, productivity gains, more competitive wages and lower indirect taxes can result in increased output and lower unemployment in parallel to the deflation. This type of deflation is very much desirable.

In the graph below, this is illustrated by movement from SRAS 1 to SRAS 2 as costs of production fall.

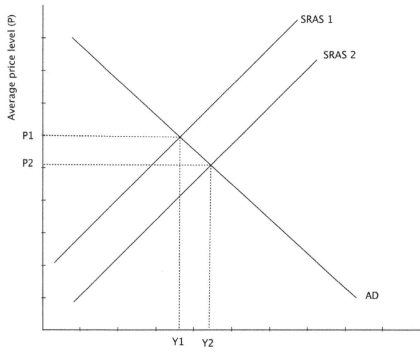

Numerical application:
Construct a weighted price index from data
Calculate inflation using price index and base year

- **Inflation/ Unemployment trade-off**

With a standard set of AD and AS curves there is an inverse relationship between inflation and unemployment (as output rises, it is assumed that unemployment falls). Keynesian economists, based on their view of the AS curve, theorise that increases in AD would reduce unemployment because at low levels of output spare capacity means that prices are stable. It would be as the economy neared full employment inflation would start to increase.

In 1958 A. W. Phillips' study of 95 years of unemployment and inflation data suggested an inverse relationship and led to the development of the **Phillips Curve**.

In the following diagram, AD is increased from AD1 to AD2 (equilibrium from A to B), with output increasing from Y1 to Y2 (unemployment falling) and the price level rising from P1 to P2:

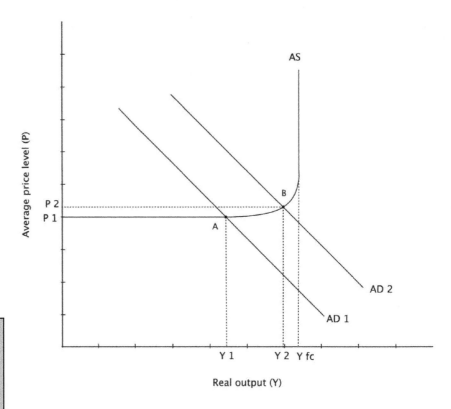

The Phillips curve below then illustrates this 'inverse' relationship with a choice of inflation/unemployment combinations at A and B.

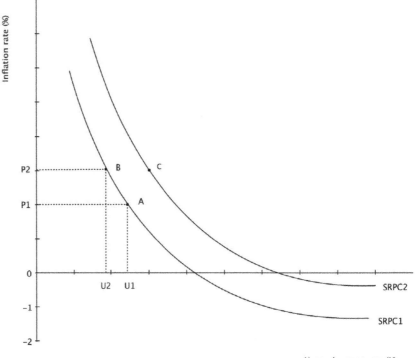

This 'relationship' broke down in the late 1960s and early 1970s when **stagflation** (**stag**nation, hence rising unemployment with rising in**flation**) appeared in most developed/ industrial economies. This is illustrated by the movement from A to C in the diagram above. Rising factor costs and oil prices fuelled rising inflation, and the situation was made worse by government policies aimed at increasing AD, to cure rising levels of unemployment.

It was soon suggested that the 'inverse' relationship between inflation and unemployment was in reality more complex, and **Milton Friedman** argued that the trade-off between inflation and unemployment only existed in the short run. Government policy to increase AD in order to reduce unemployment would only be successful in the short run, but higher inflation would eventually result with a return to higher unemployment in the long run. Increasing rates of both inflation and unemployment are represented by an outward shift in the short-run Phillips curve (SRPC1 to SRPC2 to SRPC3). In the long run, unemployment would remain stuck at **the natural rate of unemployment**. This is *the level of unemployment that exists at full employment*, i.e. at the long-run vertical AS curve. The solution here is the use of **supply-side** policies to reduce the natural rate of unemployment.

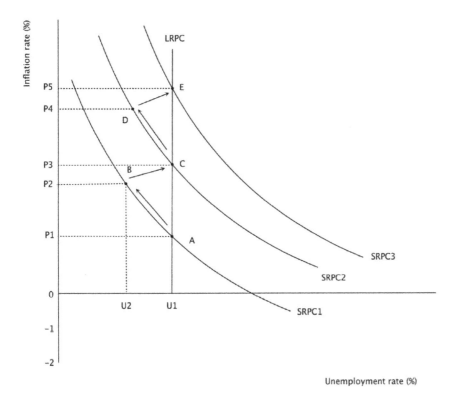

> The area of inflation/unemployment trade-off is a difficult one. It is best to base your ideas around the short-run and the long-run AS curves. Increases in AD to reduce unemployment will not cause accelerating inflation while on a SRAS. But at full employment and the LRAS any increase in AD will be purely inflationary and therefore supply-side policies should be used.

In the diagram above, a government decides to move from A to B (reducing unemployment by increasing AD from AD1 to AD2 in the diagram below). The trade-off here is a higher rate of inflation (P2). Wages rise to compensate for the higher prices, and this causes an increase in the costs of production. This decreases SRAS1 to SRAS2, resulting in a higher average price level. Output falls back to Y1, and unemployment returns to the natural rate at U1.

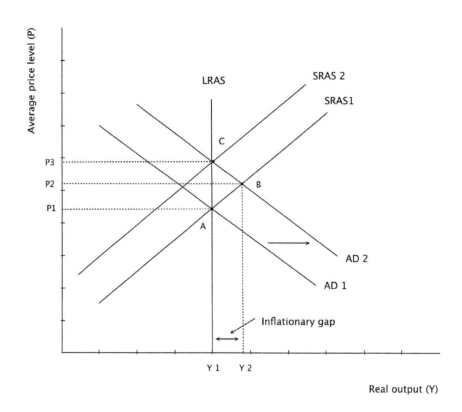

ECONOMIC GROWTH

Economic Growth *is an increase in **real** GDP over a given time period.*

It is important that you can distinguish between **actual** and **potential** growth.

Actual growth happens when an economy is below full employment and moves towards full employment by improving the use of existing resources (AD1 to AD2 in the diagram below).

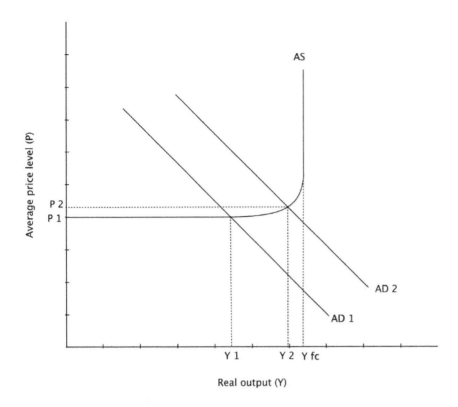

In the diagram above, with AD1 to AD2, the economy grows from Y1 to Y2. This is the same as the move from A to B in the PPC diagram below, with fewer resources unemployed at B than at A.

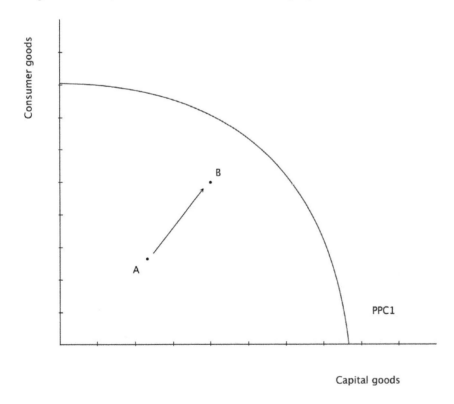

Potential growth is the long-term trend rate of growth (LRAS1 to LRAS2 in the diagram below). An increase in the quantity and/or quality of factors will result in **potential growth**. This type of growth occurs in the long run with an increase in the full employment level of income (Y1 to Y2 and PPC1 to PPC2 in the diagrams below) or potential level of output.

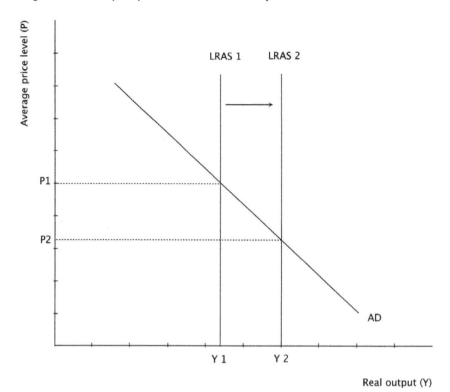

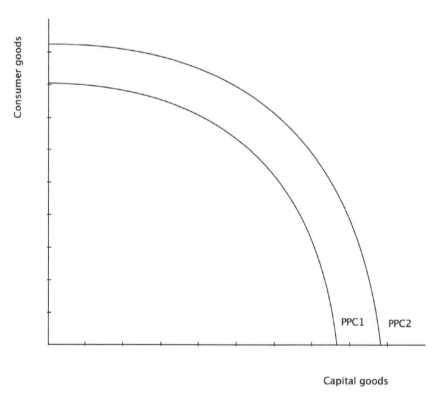

Key causes of this long run growth are investment in both physical and human capital resulting in productivity growth (output per unit of factor input).

- **Consequences of economic growth**

Benefits of growth:
- Per capita income growth and increased consumption
- Higher living standards
- Fiscal dividend (reduced government spending and increased tax revenue)
- Reduced unemployment/increased employment
- Easier to redistribute income/care for the environment

Costs of growth:
- Inflation
- Externalities and resource depletion
- Increased importing and current account deficit
- Unbalanced growth from a focus on consumption
- Unequal distribution of income

Numerical application:
Calculate change in GDP
Calculate % change in real GDP (using a price index)

> **DISTRIBUTION OF INCOME**

Income is unequally distributed within economies, and whilst inequality does provide some useful functions, such as providing incentives and rewards, there is a broad acceptance of the need for redistribution from rich to poor. Where the disagreement lies is in the amount of redistribution that should take place, and by what means. Any analysis of income distribution needs to consider whether taxes have been removed and benefits been added.

- **Measuring the distribution of income**

A **Lorenz curve** *shows the proportion of a nation's income that is earned by any given percentage of the population.*

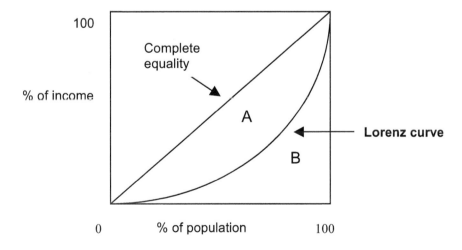

The curve is below the line of complete equality because, for example, the poorest 20% of the population will own less than 20% of national income. The more 'bowed' the line, the greater the degree of inequality.

The **Gini coefficient** gives a numerical measure to the degree of inequality (the higher the number the greater the inequality).

$$\text{Gini coefficient} = \frac{A}{A+B}$$

Incomes differ for a wide variety of reasons including: labour market conditions, bargaining power, tax and benefit structures, wealth, discrimination, household composition, qualifications and hours worked.

- **Government tax and benefit measures to redistribute income**
  By using the tax and benefit system, governments can redistribute income from rich to poor. For example, progressive income taxes will take income from the rich that can then be redistributed using **transfer payments** *(income transferred from one person to another without any production taking place)* such as unemployment benefit or pensions.

  Taxes can be **progressive** *(the average rate of tax rises as income rises)* **regressive** *(the average rate of tax falls as income rises)* or **proportionate** *(the average rate of tax is constant).*

  Direct taxes *are taxes on income and wealth that are paid directly to tax authorities.* **Indirect taxes** *are taxes on spending that are paid by suppliers and therefore not directly by consumers.*

  Direct taxes tend to be progressive and indirect taxes tend to be regressive. Any movement away from direct to indirect taxation will therefore tend to make the distribution of income less equal.

  Other methods of promoting equity are based on government intervention to promote health care and education services (often through direct provision or subsidies), clean water and sanitation, as well as other basic infrastructures.

- **Poverty**
  Most countries have a level of income that is defined as a 'poverty line' (set at a level that is the minimum needed for basic needs), and if a family has an income that is below this then they are in **absolute poverty**. The World Bank defines 'extreme poverty' as living on less than $1.25 a day. **Relative poverty** compares incomes in a country with median incomes (a measure of income needed for a lifestyle typical for a certain society and above absolute poverty).

Causes of poverty:
- Low incomes
- Unemployment
- Unequal distribution of ownership of land and resources
- Age, gender and other forms of discrimination
- Lack of human capital
- Poverty cycles

Consequences of poverty:
- Social problems
- Lack of access to health care and education
- Low living standards
- Higher levels of preventable disease and illness, infant mortality, child and maternal mortality

---

Numerical application:
Calculate marginal and average tax rates
Calculate tax payable at a given level of income

Macroeconomics is examined in Paper 1 (extended response/essay) Section B.

1. (a) Explain why a country may wish to reduce its inflation rate.
(10 marks)

   (b) Evaluate the likely effects on an economy of relying on demand-side policies to reduce the rate of inflation.
(15 marks)

2. (a) Explain how fiscal policy can be used to make supply-side improvements to an economy.
(10 marks)

   (b) Evaluate the use of supply-side policies to increase Gross Domestic Product (GDP).
(15 marks)

Model markschemes to these questions are on pages 126-40.

SECTION 3: INTERNATIONAL ECONOMICS

REASONS FOR TRADE

Countries trade because there are **gains** from doing so:
- Specialisation and comparative advantage
- Increased choice
- Lower costs
- Lower prices
- Gains from competition
- Economies of scale
- Increased efficiency in the allocation of resources
- Source of foreign exchange

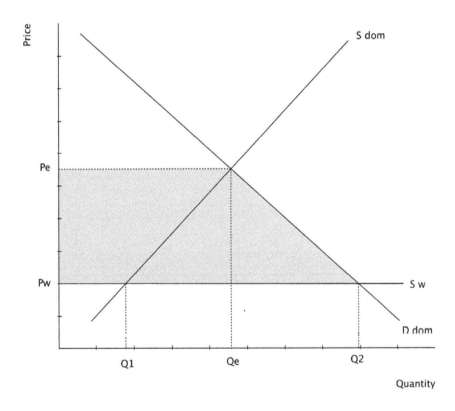

In the diagram above, the shaded area represents the increase in consumer surplus from trade. The world price (Pw) is below the domestic equilibrium price (Pe) and imports are Q1 (domestic quantity supplied) to Q2 (domestic quantity demanded).

Absolute Advantage

Absolute advantage exists *if a country can produce a good using fewer resources than another country.*

Comparative Advantage

Here the cost is an opportunity cost, NOT a monetary cost. The distinction becomes clear when you realise that comparative advantage graphs and numerical examples are just examples of Production Possibilities Frontiers.

Comparative advantage exists *if a country can produce a good at a lower **opportunity cost** than another country*. Countries have differing factor endowments, and if countries specialise in goods in which they have a comparative advantage, then world output will increase and countries will be able to consume beyond their Production Possibilities Frontier (given certain assumptions). Even if a country has an absolute advantage, this will still be true.

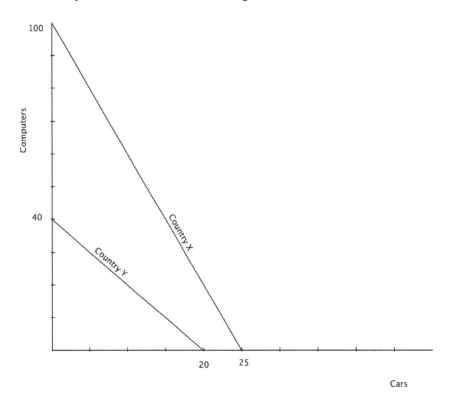

	Computers	Cars
X	100	25
Y	40	20

Both the diagram and the table above show the production possibilities of countries X and Y with a given set of resources. Here country X has an absolute advantage in both goods (it can produce more of both goods with the same resources as Y). From the graph we can see that the **opportunity costs** of production of each good differ in each country because the PPFs are not parallel. X has a comparative advantage in computers and Y has a comparative advantage in cars.

In X:

the opportunity cost of producing 1 computer is $^1/_4$ of a car (100/100 -> 25/100)
the opportunity cost of producing 1 car is 4 computers (25/25 ->100/25)

In Y:

the opportunity cost of producing 1 computer is $^1/_2$ of a car (40/40 -> 20/40)

the opportunity cost of producing 1 car is 2 computers
(20/20 -> 40/20)

So if country X can buy cars from Y for less than 4 computers and Y can sell cars to X for more than 2 computers then both countries will gain. If country Y can buy computers for less than ½ car and country X can sell computers for more than ¼ car then both countries will gain.

Here the **terms of trade** will be 1 car : 3 computers.

The above model is based on the following **assumptions**:
- Two countries and two products
- Each country has a given set of resources
- Perfect factor mobility
- No transport costs
- Constant returns to scale
- No externalities from production

Comparative advantage is **limited** by the existence of barriers to trade in the real world, it ignores transport costs, it assumes perfect factor mobility and the fact that specialisation could cause either economies or diseconomies of scale.

> **Numerical application:**
> Calculate opportunity cost from data or graph to determine comparative advantage

TERMS OF TRADE

Terms of Trade *measure the rate at which one good is exchanged for another.*

Index of Terms of Trade = $\frac{\text{Index of Export Prices}}{\text{Index of Import Prices}} \times 100$

An **improvement in the terms of trade** *means that export prices have risen relative to import prices.*

Changes in the terms of trade have impacts both on an economy's domestic economy and on the balance of payments. Non-oil exporting developing countries have faced falling terms of trade and so ELDCs have had to sell greater quantities of exports in order to pay for imports. ELDCs tend to produce and export primary products which have a low income elasticity of demand. On the other hand, they tend to import manufactured goods that have a higher positive income elasticity of demand, so as world income increases, demand-side factors increase the price of manufactured goods faster than primary products. On the supply side, developed economies have overproduced agricultural goods (especially through the CAP in the EU) and this oversupply has further depressed primary product prices. With the demand for primary products being price inelastic, any increase in supply will have a stronger depressing effect on prices.

The effect on the balance of payments will depend upon the price elasticities of demand for exports and imports (see Marshall-Lerner condition, page 102).

Numerical applications:
Calculate terms of trade index from an export price index and an import price index
Calculate (percentage) the extent of an improvement or deterioration in the terms of trade

---

● The World Trade organization (WTO)
The WTO deals with global 'rules' governing trade between different economies/countries. It has an overall aim to increase trade between countries by lowering trade barriers and easing the general flow of trade.

WTO functions:
- Execute and administer WTO agreements between members
- Provide a forum for trade negotiation
- Rule on trade disputes between member countries
- Monitor member trade policies
- Provide assistance for ELDCs on trade issues

Much of this work is carried out in cooperation with other international organizations such as the IMF and the World Bank.

FREE TRADE/PROTECTIONISM

Free trade *is the international exchange of goods and services without any artificial* **barriers to trade** *(actions taken by governments to either restrict imports or promote domestic production and exports).*

Arguments for protectionism:
- Infant industry argument
- Anti-dumping
- Protecting employment
- Balance of Payments
- Externalities and demerit goods
- Strategic/security reasons
- Unrealistic assumptions of comparative advantage

Arguments against protectionism:
- Loss of comparative advantage
- Costs to consumers/producers
- Increased prices/costs of importing
- Loss of competitiveness and efficiency
- Governments choose the wrong areas to protect
- Retaliation and trade wars
- Misallocation of resources

- **Tariffs**

A tax on imports both restricts imports and raises revenue for the government.

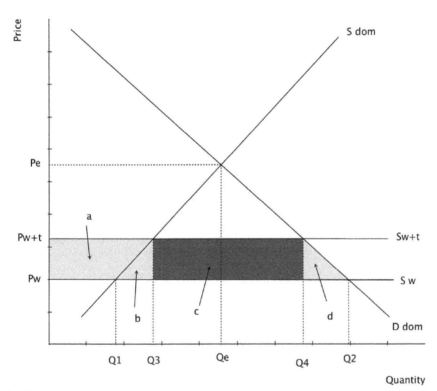

In the graph above, D and S represent domestic demand for and domestic supply of a particular good, and the pre-trade equilibrium is at (Pe,Qe). The world price of this good (P_W) is lower that the price of domestically-produced goods (Pe), and so quantity demanded increases from Qe to Q_2 and the quantity supplied by domestic firms falls to Q_1. This shortfall (Q_1 to Q_2) is covered by imports. Then this country decides to put a tariff on imports and this increases the price of imports (P_{W+T}), thus reducing the quantity demanded to Q_4 and increasing the quantity supplied by domestic firms to Q_3. This reduced shortfall is covered by a reduced number of imports (Q_3 to Q_4).

The shaded (light and dark) trapezium represents the loss of consumer surplus from the tariff (caused by the increase in price). This area can be divided into the following 'sub areas' that explain what has happened to that 'lost' consumer surplus: 'a' is the addition to domestic producer surplus, 'c' (dark shaded area) is the tariff revenue gained by the government, and both 'b' and 'd' represent the deadweight welfare loss from the tariff.

The final effects of a tariff will depend upon the price elasticities of demand and supply and the size of the tariff itself.

- ● **Quotas**

A **quota** *is a physical limit on imports in terms of volume or value.*

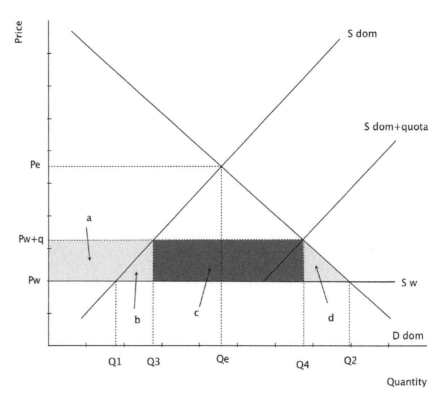

The graph above shows how the restriction on imports (quota) increases the price of imports. This essentially has the same impact as a tariff by increasing the quantity supplied by domestic suppliers (Q1 to Q3) and reducing the quantity demanded by domestic consumers (Q2 to Q4), thus reducing imports to Q3 to Q4. This time, area 'c' is the revenue gained by the importing firms from overseas, who are able to import under the quota system at higher prices.

- ● **Subsidies**

A subsidy lowers the production costs for domestic producers but does not alter the market price. In the graph below, with lower production costs (vertical distance between S dom and S dom+sub), domestic producers increase supply (S dom+sub). Imports fall to Q3 to Q2 (from Q1 to Q2) and domestic firms' revenue rises from box 'a' (pre-subsidy) to 'a'+'b'+'e'. Importers now have a revenue of just 'c'+'d'. The shaded area 'e' represents the monetary cost of the subsidy to the government. Triangle 'f' represents the inefficiency caused by the misallocation of resources away from a low cost producer (importers) to a high cost producer (domestic producers).

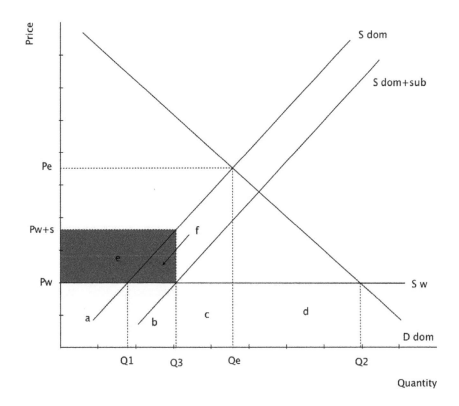

- ● **Administrative Barriers**

Countries can make it difficult to import goods by using bureaucratic delays and tight safety restrictions

---

Numerical application:
Calculate from diagrams the effects of a tariff, quota and subsidy on all stakeholders (domestic consumers and producers, foreign producers and the government)
Calculate the change in net welfare

ECONOMIC INTEGRATION

Globalization, as defined by the OECD, is *'the geographical dispersion of industrial and service activities and the cross-border networking of companies'*. The rate of growth of international trade far exceeds the rate of growth of world output. This process has been happening for many centuries, but today's communications systems and the growth of MNCs/TNCs have accelerated the pace of globalisation.

- ● **Preferential trade agreements**

These are where two or more countries agree to remove or reduce artificial trade barriers such as tariffs between themselves. The 'preferential' element of this agreement involves countries buying imports from a country in the agreement rather than from a lower cost producer outside the agreement. These agreements can be bilateral or multilateral. Currently Chile and India have a bilateral agreement on goods. An example of a multilateral agreement is the Melanesian Spearhead Group (Fiji, Papua New Guinea, Solomon Island and Vanatu).

• Trading Blocs

A **Free Trade Area** is created *when countries form a trading area within which they move goods and services freely but each individual country retains its own barriers to outside countries.*

In a **Customs Union** *individual country trade barriers no longer exist and there is a unified trade policy.*

A **Common Market** is *a customs union with the free movement of factors of production as well.*

Customs Unions may cause either **Trade Creation** *(a shift of production from high-cost to low-cost countries)* or **Trade Diversion** *(a shift in production from low-cost countries outside the union to high-cost, although tariff-free, countries inside the union).*

The reluctance to surrender both political and economic sovereignty may act as a barrier to further integration.

• Monetary union

This is a common market with a common currency and a common central bank (eg. the Eurozone)

Advantages:
- Resource allocation more efficient
- Increased real incomes/quality of life
- Increased export markets/ease of trade
- Price transparency
- Coordinated macro policy with lower inflation and interest rates
- Increased inward investment
- Reduced ER uncertainty between members

Disadvantages:
- Increased competition costs
- With lower levels of integration, firms may exploit differences in employment and environmental legislation
- Loss of economic sovereignty (especially monetary policy)
- 'One size fits all' nature of monetary policy
- Problems dealing with asymmetric shocks

EXCHANGE RATES

An **exchange rate** is *the price of one currency in terms of another.*

- **Floating Exchange Rates**

Here the value of a currency is solely determined by the forces of demand and supply. There is no target exchange rate set by the government and there is no government intervention in foreign currency markets.

The **demand** for a currency is based upon:
- The demand for exports of goods and services
- Inflows of direct and portfolio investment
- Speculative buying
- Central Bank officially buying the currency

The **supply** of a currency is based upon:
- The demand for imported goods and services
- Outflows of direct and portfolio investment
- Speculative selling
- Central Bank officially selling the currency

Your work on exchange rates should be structured around a clear understanding of the factors that determine the demand for, and supply of, a currency. As with a normal market, a clear understanding of the determinants of market forces will enable you to apply your knowledge to a variety of situations.

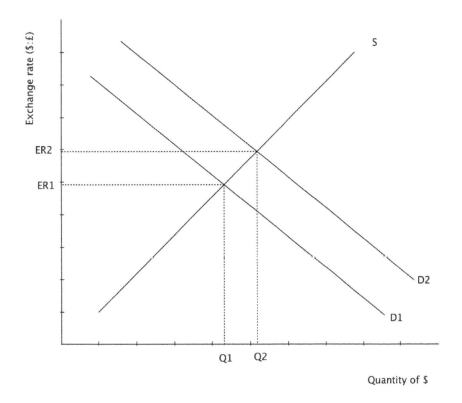

As the above graph shows, currency will appreciate as the demand for it increases (D_1 to D_2).

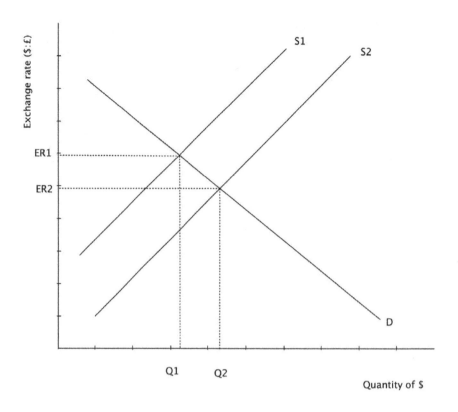

A currency will depreciate as the supply of it increases (S_1 to S_2), as indicated in the graph above.

Factors that change a floating exchange rate:
- **Monetary Policy.** Investors move funds around the world in search of the highest rates of return. Relatively high rates of interest attract funds and so increase the demand for a currency
- **Fiscal Policy.** Countries with sound public finances will tend to see their currencies appreciate
- **Growth.** Increase in national income may increase the demand for imports and therefore depreciate a currency. But slow growth is a sign of economic weakness, and this will also depreciate a currency
- **Inflation.** Countries with relatively high rates of inflation will see a loss in export competitiveness and imports becoming relatively cheaper. A downward pressure will be brought to bear on their exchange rate. Purchasing Power Parity Theory suggests that exchange rates will adjust to reflect the differences in inflation rates between countries. This will equalise the real purchasing power in each country
- **Trade Balance.** A trade surplus will tend to cause an exchange rate to rise, and a deficit will tend to cause an exchange rate to fall
- **Speculation.** This can have a huge impact on the value of a currency

- **Managed Floating Exchange Rates (managed float)**
Here the exchange rate is determined by the forces of demand and supply, but governments (central banks) aim to limit

fluctuations and might 'manage' the value of the currency to achieve a macroeconomic goal such as low inflation or to stimulate export growth.

- **Fixed Exchange Rate**

Here the exchange rate cannot fluctuate from the central rate – it is 'pegged' to another currency. The exchange rate will then have a specific target and will be a dominant part of economic policy. The government will intervene to maintain the value of the currency using the rate of interest and/or currency reserves.

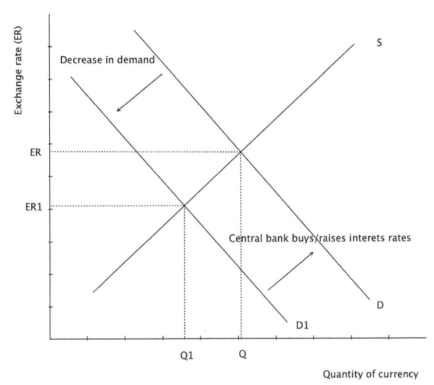

Quantity of currency

In the graph above, the central bank responds to a fall in demand by buying the currency and/or raising interest rates.

In China the government has used a variety of methods to sustain a low fixed exchange rate in order to maintain export competitiveness.

In Argentina the government has used a variety of methods to sustain a high fixed exchange rate in order to reduce the rate of inflation.

- **Common Currencies and Monetary Integration**

Here, countries replace their national currencies with a common currency. The best example of this is the Euro, where monetary policy, controlled by a single central bank, covers all countries (the ECB).

Advantages of a floating exchange rate:
- No need for currency reserves
- Monetary policy free to target domestic goals

- Automatic balance of payments adjustment
- Reduced risk of speculation

Advantages of fixed exchange rates:
- Inflation discipline
- Certainty through currency stability increases trade
- Reduces costs of currency hedging for firms

Advantages of a strong currency:
- Reduced import costs
- Inflationary discipline
- Improvement in the terms of trade
- Increased real purchasing power abroad

Disadvantages of a strong currency:
- Increased import penetration
- Exports struggle to maintain competitiveness
- Reduces economic growth
- Asymmetrical effects on regions and sectors

> The disadvantages of each system are the opposite of the advantages of the alternative system. For example, a floating exchange rate does not provide inflation discipline, and a fixed exchange rate requires currency reserves.

Depreciation vs. devaluation

A **depreciation** is the fall in value of a currency in a floating exchange rate system caused by movements in the demand for and supply of the currency. A **devaluation** is the fall in the value of a currency in a fixed exchange rate system after a conscious decision by a government to reduce the value of its currency.

Appreciation vs. revaluation

An **appreciation** is the rise in value of a currency in a floating exchange rate system caused by movements in the demand for and supply of the currency. A **revaluation** is the rise in the value of a currency in a fixed exchange rate system after a conscious decision by a government to increase the value of its currency.

Numerical application:
Calculate changes in the value of a currency from a set of data
Calculate and exchange rate from data and using linear demand and supply functions plotted from data
Calculate, using exchange rates, the price of a good in different currencies

---

BALANCE OF PAYMENTS

The **Balance of Payments** *is an account of a country's financial transactions with the rest of the world.* The **current account** measures *the value of trade in goods and services and net investment income and transfers.* The **capital and financial accounts** measure *capital flows (shares, government debt and foreign investment).*

The Balance of Payments must balance. If a country runs a current account deficit then this must be funded by a financial/capital account surplus. This surplus can either come from foreign direct investment, attracting short-term inflows of funds through attractive rates of interest, or from the selling of government foreign currency reserves.

Current account:
- Balance of trade in goods
- Balance of trade in services
- Income
- Current transfers

Capital account:
- Capital transfers
- Transactions in non-produced, non-financial assets

Financial account:
- Direct investment
- Portfolio investment
- Reserve assets

Current account = capital account + financial account + errors and omissions

- **Current account deficit**

When the total value of an economy's exports of goods and services is less than the total value of imports of goods and services from the rest of the world (including income and transfers).

A deficit will, other things being equal, exert a downward pressure on an economy's exchange rate.

Implications of a persistent current account deficit:
- Ownership of financial and capital assets transfers overseas
- Downward pressure on ER. This is inflationary, and the central bank may need to respond by raising interest rates
- Opportunity costs of debt funding
- Effects on credit rating

- **Current account surplus**

When the total value of an economy's exports of goods and services is greater than the total value of imports of goods and services from the rest of the world (including income and transfers).

A surplus will (other things being equal) exert an upward pressure on an economy's exchange rate.

Implications of a persistent current account surplus:
* Risk of protectionist measures for deficit countries
* Upward pressure on the currency

Numerical Application:
Calculate the balance of payments from data

CORRECTING A CURRENT ACCOUNT DEFICIT

• Changes in the Exchange Rate
A devaluation of an exchange rate will make exports more competitive and imports more expensive and vice versa.

The final impact of a devaluation on the balance of payments will depend upon the **Marshall-Lerner condition** *(a devaluation in the exchange rate will improve the balance of payments if the sum of the price elasticities and demand for exports and imports is greater than 1).* A devaluation might take time to have a positive effect on the balance of payments, and it might even make thing worse initially, because of the **'J' curve** effect. It takes time for traders to adjust to new prices and so the Marshall-Lerner condition is not immediately satisfied.

• Changes in Aggregate Demand
There is obviously a strong link between international trade and
    $$AD=C+I+G+(X-M).$$
An increase in export revenues will increase AD, and an increase in expenditure on imports will decrease AD.

For a country with a high marginal propensity to import, an increase in AD will increase import expenditure and so move the balance of payments towards a deficit.

• Protectionism
A country with a fixed exchange rate will not be able to rely upon a devaluation in order to improve the competitiveness of its exports and so it might well have to consider protectionist measures to attempt to improve its balance of payments.

- **Supply-side policies**

These aim to increase the productive potential of an economy, enabling it competitively to produce goods for which there is an international market. These are policies that encourage resources to be mobile towards goods and services that are in demand, and the development of areas where comparative advantage exists. Other policies that encourage investment, innovation, competition and flexible factor payments (especially wages) are key areas for policy focus.

- **Expenditure Switching and Expenditure Changing**

Under a managed exchange rate system there are some long-term options for making balance of payments adjustments:

Expenditure switching aims to encourage domestic consumers to switch expenditure from imports to domestic goods using policies such as protectionism, devaluation (see Marshall-Lerner condition and the 'J' curve) and increasing competitiveness.

Expenditure changing aims to reduce aggregate demand (especially for countries with a high marginal propensity to import) and so reduce expenditure on imports by using fiscal and monetary policies to influence AD.

- **Persistent Current Account Deficits**

A deficit is caused by **cyclical and structural factors** and a persistent deficit will tend to be caused by structural factors. An economy might have a problem with its competitiveness or it simply may not produce the type of goods that are needed by its domestic consumers or in export markets. In a floating exchange rate system the currency will depreciate, but in a fixed exchange rate system this is not an option. Here the government will have to encourage inflows on the capital account and buy up excess foreign currency. This can only happen in the short term, as it requires foreign currency reserves to be used.

A country might improve its international competitiveness by increasing productivity, reducing the costs of production, devaluing the currency, improving the quality of output, encouraging investment and innovation, and stimulating competition by reducing protectionist measures.

- **Persistent Current Account Surplus**

If a country imports far less than it exports (China) then this essentially means that a country is not using the total value of its national income to consume. The surplus national income is then 'saved' by buying overseas financial and physical capital (a financial account inflow for countries with a current account deficit), thus funding current accounts deficits in other countries. There will, of course, be upward pressure on the surplus country's exchange rate. However, China maintains a 'weak' RMB in the forex markets.

International Economics is examined in Paper 2 (data response) Section A.

1. (a) Define the following terms:

      (i)   Exchange rate   (2 marks)

      (ii)   Appreciation   (2 marks)

  (b) Using an appropriate diagram, explain how increased spending on food imports could affect an exchange rate.

                                            (4 marks)

  (c) Using an appropriate diagram, explain how the continuing increase in prices for imported raw materials could affect the general price level and output.   (4 marks)

  (d) Using information from the text/data and your knowledge of economics, evaluate the impact on an economy of the decision to introduce tariffs.   (8 marks)

Data responses are questions that are based upon text and data, which are not included here. There is more information on this with the model markschemes at the end of the book.

SECTION 4: DEVELOPMENT ECONOMICS

Many economic models that appear in the section on Development Economics have already appeared in earlier sections of this guide (as they do in the syllabus). You should seek to apply these concepts to development issues, thus giving a topic that is often seen as not having a theory structure behind it a clear structure for economic analysis and evaluation.

Theory already highlighted in the micro part of the course:
- Prices: volatile commodity prices, PED/PES
- Externalities: education (+ve) and environmental damage (-ve)
- Merit goods
- Public good and common resource issues
- PPC – investment
- Opportunity cost

Theory already highlighted in the macro part of the course:
- Sources of growth
- Factor endowments and global inequality
- Gains from trade
- Problems with trade and trade barriers
- Measuring GDP etc
- Income inequality and Lorenz curves/Gini coefficients
- Government policies to targets growth (demand and supply-side)

> Development Economics is a dangerous area for most students, because they forget all the pure theories and concepts around which good economics is structured. Instead, Development Economics tends to slide into an unstructured mass of anecdotal stories that do little to explain, analyse and evaluate the problems experienced by developing economies. Good Development Economics will make use of as many economic concepts as any other area of the syllabus. To help you with this, economic concepts are highlighted in **bold type**.

INTRODUCTION TO DEVELOPMENT

Distinction between Growth and Development

Growth is not the same as development. **Growth**, measured in terms of *an increase in GDP*, is a **quantitative** measure.
Real GDP per capita figures are an inadequate means of making comparisons both within countries and between countries.

Limitations of GDP as a measure to compare welfare between countries:
- The 'shadow' economy often means that GDP calculations are an underestimation of actual GDP
- Regional variations exist within countries
- Externalities are unaccounted for
- New products and improvements in quality are unaccounted for

- Some countries have more leisure time for similar levels of GDP
- Currencies in one country may not have the same purchasing power as in another country and so a common currency ($) may be used to make comparisons
- Even with a common currency not all goods are traded, products are regionally differentiated, there are local taxes, and currencies fluctuate

Development is a **qualitative** *measure of an improvement in the quality of life*. An economy can grow without developing and an economy can develop without growth, however in the long run, economic growth is usually a necessary condition for development.

Economic development is a broad concept involving:
- Improvement in the standard of living
- Reduction in poverty
- Improved health care and education
- Reduction in underemployment
- Greater income distribution equality
- Increased freedom and choice
- Environmental protection

Characteristics of Economic Growth

- **Variations in long-run growth rates**

Given compound **growth rates**, small differences in annual growth rates can open up wide gaps in growth and income between countries. Poor countries find it easier to achieve high growth rates than rich countries, as they are growing from comparatively low levels of income. Growth also needs to take into account changes in population (**GDP per capita**).

- **Changes associated with economic growth**
  - Primary $\Rightarrow$ Secondary $\Rightarrow$ Tertiary (changes driven by income elasticity of demand)
  - Urbanisation
  - Growth of GDP per capita
  - Increased productivity
  - Increased international trade

- **Pollution and environmental degradation**

All economies damage the environment as they grow. Developed economies, with high levels of consumption demand, cause environmental damage, as do countries developing from modest foundations. **Deforestation** caused by clearing for farmland, timber use for fuel and exportation causes soil erosion and contributes to global warming and a **loss of biodiversity**. Over-farming leads to **soil degradation**. **Hazardous waste** products are generated by unregulated industries and slums. **Polluted water** generates disease. **Air pollution** is caused by lack of government controls on pollution, overpopulation and the burning for fuel of polluting materials. Carbon dioxide emissions deplete the ozone layer, causing **global warming**.

- **Income inequality**

If **growth** rather than development is prioritised, **investment** has a central part to play. In order for investment to occur there needs to be saving by a high-income sector, and this requires an unequal distribution of income. In most ELDCs the richest 10% of the population own 40-50% of the total national income.

- **Sustainable development**

Sustainable development means that *economic growth in the short run must not compromise the ability of an economy in the long run to meet the needs of future generations.*

At the moment many of our actions, particularly those that are permanent and irreversible, are limiting the actions of future generations. The problem is that whilst a majority of pollution is caused by highly industrialised economies, serious and unsustainable environmental consequences will be experienced if ELDCs use the same industrial techniques. But if ELDCs have to develop in a more sustainable way, their growth and development will be hampered and slowed.

Solutions:
- Government provision of basic sanitation and clean water
- Extension of property rights
- Prohibition of polluting activities
- Pollution taxes
- Tradable pollution permits
- Finding environmental actions that actually promote growth
- Education of farmers and communities
- Family planning
- Removal of subsidies that encourage the use of fossil fuels

Whilst it is dangerous to generalise, there are **Common characteristics of ELDCs:**
- Low levels of GDP per capita
- High levels of poverty
- Relatively large agricultural/primary sectors
- Large informal/imperfect markets
- High birth rates
- Low levels of productivity
- High levels of unemployment/underemployment
- Dominated/dependent upon developed economies

There are also key areas that represent causes of **diversity between ELDCs:**
- Historical background (colonisation is a big issue here)
- Resource endowment and geographical factors
- Political structures
- Industrial structure (primary/secondary/tertiary)
- Ethnic/religious factors

- **Poverty cycle/trap**

Low income $\Rightarrow$ low savings (in order to save a surplus is required and this is difficult to generate with low incomes and subsistence living) $\Rightarrow$ low investment (the forgoing of current consumption in order to increase future consumption; this forgoing of consumption is not possible in subsistence economies) $\Rightarrow$ low income $\Rightarrow$ etc.

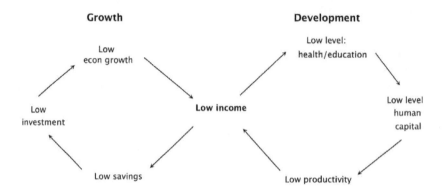

- **International development goals**

There are eight UN Millennium Development Goals (adopted in 2000 by 189 countries and aimed to be achieved by 2015). They are to:
- Eradicate extreme poverty and hunger
- Achieve universal primary education
- Promote gender equality and empower women
- Reduce child mortality rate
- Improve maternal health
- Combat HIV/AIDS, malaria, and other diseases
- Ensure environmental sustainability
- Develop a global partnership for development

MEASURING DEVELOPMENT

Indicators of Development

- **Indicators**

As development is so hard to define, a variety of indicators can be used:

Monetary/financial:
- <u>GNP/GDP</u>

- **GNP/GDP per capita** (low-, middle- and high-income countries). These figures are limited in their use, eg. income distribution
- Use of **PPP** to make comparisons for GNP/GDP per capita

Health:
- **Birth rates** in ELDCs tend to be double those in developed countries
- **Life expectancy at birth** is the number of years that a newborn baby can expect to live given constant health standards, and is much lower in ELDCs
- **Infant mortality rates** measure the number of deaths per 1000 under the age of one year (not including babies born dead)
- **Population growth** tends to be high in ELDCs, because of poverty, and the age structure is weighted towards the young

Education:
- **Literacy rates** are a problem for ELDCs
- **Net primary education enrolment**
- **Primary teacher/pupil ratio**

These are not an exhaustive list of possible indicators and you should feel free to develop an understanding of ELDCs through a variety of different measures.

The key thing that you must be able to do is to **compare and contrast figures**, for all the above underlined headings (including HDI data) for economically more developed and economically less developed countries.

● Composite Indicators
The **Human Development Index** (HDI) is seen as a method of overcoming issues that surround the use of single indicators. It combines **GNP per capita, life expectancy and literacy rates**, and shows that growth does not necessarily equate with development. There are countries with low GNP per capita and yet a high HDI, and vice versa.

You must be able to **compare and contrast HDI figures** for economically more developed and economically less developed countries.

Often countries have different global rankings for GDP/GNI per capital in comparison to their global ranking for HDI. Kuwait is a good country to illustrate such differences in ranking (5th for GDP per capital and 45th for HDI). These differences can be explained by political factors and the choices that policymakers make in terms of prioritising growth and development. Some countries clearly underperform in HDI terms in relation to their income levels.

DOMESTIC FACTORS

• **Education and health**

People create wealth. An expanding population might mean a plentiful **labour supply** but it will also tend to reduce **GNP per capita**. The quality of labour is important and so **investment** in education, training and health care needs to take place – but it involves an **opportunity cost**. **Entrepreneurs** are also needed. Social and cultural barriers often exist and inhibit change, new methods of working, and a more scientific approach to production. There is very strong statistical evidence of the link between education/health and income growth. Health is a clear improvement of the quality of life and enables individuals to have a more consistent working life. Both factors enable workers to be more productive.

In the provision of both education and health care there is often a high degree of opportunity cost for governments, and also for families 'releasing' children from work to education.

• **Appropriate technology**

Investment is *the forgoing of current consumption for increased future consumption*. Technological change and capital investment often go hand-in-hand. Development depends upon **appropriate technology**, enabling ELDCs to focus on reducing poverty instead of simply enabling income to increase.

• **Credit and micro-credit**

Investment cannot take place unless there is saving, but **saving** requires there to be surplus income. Financial institutions such as stock exchanges, savings and investment banks play an important role in channelling savings towards investment opportunities. These often do not effectively exist for small firms and farms, and this is where a large part of economic activity happens in ELDCs and where inroads can be made into poverty.

Micro-credit schemes are systems of small loans for income-generating activities (eg. fish farming, mat-weaving, small-scale retailing and brick-making) which enable poor communities in ELDCs to gain some economic stability. Schemes are planned to provide people with the resources they need without encouraging debt. Micro-credit represents a significant way in which people can make a difference to their own lives without the dependence associated with hand-outs. Credit is often only given after a period of financial and skill training has been completed, and the schemes are designed to meet the particular needs and circumstances of those individuals taking part. Schemes aim to enable communities to diversify their skills so that communities do not suffer the problems associated with an over-concentration on one particular skill. Most micro-credit institutions also encourage saving.

- **Empowerment of women**

Women are in a position to play an important role in development. The more educated women become, the lower birth rates tend to be. This reduces dependency rates and enables existing education/health/food resources to be divided among fewer people. Of course population growth rates also affect GDP per capita. Women workers are an important resource, but one which is 'underused' (in terms of the production of output) in many ELDCs.

- **Income distribution**

A highly unequal distribution of income tends to constrain growth and development because those on low incomes have a high propensity to consume (low savings results in low levels of investment) and the wealthy, gaining political power, tend to generate policies that favour the status quo. Wealthy individuals in ELDCs also tend to have a high marginal propensity to import and generate large amounts of 'capital flight'.

- **Institutional Factors**

Taxes, legal frameworks, **over-regulation**, a lack of effective **property rights** and traditional thoughts and practices can all provide the wrong incentives and act as barriers to development. Also a lack of basic infrastructure inhibits development.

Political instability, a lack of national cohesion and the cultural and economic attitudes needed for economic growth as well as the desire by developed countries to maintain the present status quo all act as barriers to growth.

In the **formal economy** *activities are recorded officially* but in many ELDCs *economic activity is often unrecorded and even illegal* and this is the **informal economy**.

INTERNATIONAL TRADE

International trade problems:

- **Over-specialisation**

Adverse movements in the **terms of trade** and protectionist measures by developed economies are both strong barriers to development. The cause of adverse movements in the **terms of trade** has already been covered. Many ELDCs also focus on a narrow range of exports.

- **Primary product price volatility**

The volatility of commodity prices has already been covered earlier in this guide. The volatility of prices will affect revenues/incomes, making investment and planning difficult for both firms and governments.

- **Inability to access international markets**

Many ELDCs are concerned that countries such as the USA and those in the European Union support **free trade** on the one hand and yet use **subsidies** and other methods as **trade barriers**. These are used to unfairly support their domestic industries with the result that world markets are flooded with surplus goods, driving prices down. Many protectionist measures that exist do so in the form of standards and regulations that are technically hard or costly for ELDCs to comply with.

Trade strategies:

- **Open, outward-oriented (export promotion) vs. closed, inward-oriented (import substitution)**

An open, outward-oriented strategy aims to encourage export production to fund imports, and a closed, inward-oriented strategy aims to discourage imports and provide domestically-produced **substitutes**.

An open, outward-oriented strategy embraces **free trade** (although facing problems caused by developed world **protectionism**), MNCs and the free movement of productive resources. Because of the problems mentioned above with primary products, exports will tend to centre on manufactured goods. This approach has been key to rapid growth rates in China and India.

In theory, countries should specialise in producing goods and services in which they have a **comparative advantage**. Practically, for most ELDCs, this means **primary goods**. Developed economies dominate world trade, with ELDCs representing around 20% of world exports (although this figure is inflated by ELDCs that export oil). A dependence on primary products has resulted in a slow growth of exports (low **YED** and **protectionism** by developed countries), fast growth of imports (high YED), and worsening **terms of trade**.

A closed, inward-oriented strategy erects **tariffs** and other protectionist measures. It does not embrace the activities of MNCs, and restricts the movement of resources. Many countries taking this approach have experienced low growth (Ghana, and many South American countries).

- **Trade liberalisation**

Moves towards 'freer' trade, it is believed, will help ELDCs focus on exporting goods and services in which they have a comparative advantage (covered earlier on in this guide).

- **The role of the WTO**

This is covered earlier on in this guide.

- **Diversification**

As already mentioned, a narrow focus on primary product exports is problematic for ELDCs. Diversification aims to move production into the secondary sector exporting manufactured/semi-manufactured goods and thus avoiding the problems of primary products. With this strategy should come higher and more stable revenues as well as gains in skill, capital investment, productivity and incomes.

- **Bilateral and regional preferential trade agreements**

These are covered earlier on in this guide.

- **Fair Trade organizations**

The 48 least-developed countries are home to 10 per cent of the world's citizens and their share of world exports has declined to 0.4 per cent over the past two decades. The USA and EU contain roughly the same number of people and account for nearly 50 per cent of world exports. Small traders find it hard to compete in a world in which trade has been 'liberalised' by the WTO. If small traders and ELDCs can be helped to overcome the significant barriers to fair trade, then trade can be a solution to slow growth and underdevelopment.

Fair Trade guarantees a price for producers that covers their costs of production and provides a sustainable living. It also provides long-term contracts and business training vital for long-term stability. Fair trade allows consumers to purchase goods that actually start to favour commodity producers in ELDCs.

FOREIGN DIRECT INVESTMENT

- **Foreign Investment (MNCs)**

FDI is often centred on the activities of MNCs (multi national corporations) who invest, in the long run, in expanding existing productive capacity or buying out existing firms overseas. These corporations do not just bring investment funds into ELDCs, but they also bring new technology, training, entrepreneurial skills (helping fill resource gaps), open new markets and have a **multiplier effect** on the wider economy. These new enterprises create jobs, generate export and tax revenue. On the other hand, **monopolistic** MNCs can be criticised for being **inefficient**, exploiting cheap labour and avoiding paying tax wherever possible as well as exploiting relaxed environmental regulations.

MNCs are attracted by new markets, natural resources, low labour, costs and regulatory frameworks that are often more 'relaxed' than in more developed countries.

Potential advantages of FDI:
- Investment in physical and financial resources overcoming the saving 'gap'
- Employment
- Training and education, expertise and R&D
- Improvements to local infrastructure
- Tax revenue
- Local multiplier effects
- Competition benefits
- Wider choice and lower prices for ELDC consumers

Potential disadvantages of FDI:
- Little impact on employment as own management teams are 'parachuted' in with impact of training thus limited
- Profits repatriated and taxes avoided
- Borrowing from ELDC financial sectors 'crowds out' local domestic investment spending
- Political power/influence over ELDC governments
- Transfer pricing to take advantage of different tax rates between countries
- Use/extract resources then leave
- Take advantage of 'relaxed' labour market and environmental regulations

AID AND MULTILATERAL ASSISTENCE

- **Aid**

Aid to ELDCs comes from two sources:
- Donor governments, called official development assistance (ODA)
- Non-governmental organisations (NGOs)

Humanitarian aid (alleviation of short-term issues and NGO priority):
- Food aid
- Medical aid
- Emergency relief aid

Development aid (long-term aid and often ODA focus):
- Grants
- Concessional long-term loans
- Project aid
- Tied aid
- Technical assistance

You need to be able to compare and contrast the nature and sources of ODA in two ELDCs.

Bilateral aid is given by individual governments and **multilateral aid** is given by multilateral agencies such as the World Bank.

Aid can help to fill **resource gaps**, which probably most often appear as a lack of capital goods. Aid can also involve developing much needed skills with which the aid itself can effectively be used. **Tied aid** is very common, and donor countries often have one eye on how they will benefit from giving aid. Aid can also delay much needed reforms, do little to reduce **income inequalities**, and support/fund dictatorships.

Grants may be used to fund specific projects or education and **soft loans** have lower rates of interest and more relaxed conditions. **Food aid** might be given using surpluses.

There are often less than ideal motives for countries giving aid, with politics and self-interest in ELDCs with abundant natural resources playing a part.

Benefits of aid:
- Fills savings and foreign exchange gaps
- Funds health/education/infrastructure
- Aids recovery from disaster

Disadvantages of aid:
- Does not reach those most in need
- ELDCs lack skills to carry out projects effectively
- Food aid causes dependency
- Tied aid
- Dependency culture develops
- Aid strengthens government control
- Industrialisation might happen too quickly
- Resources diverted away from productive sectors
- Corruption

Whilst aid might help fill in 'gaps', and certainly NGOs do provide a lot of important funds which often bypass governments and so reach the people most in need, aid is no substitute for sound economic policies and good economic management in general. Whilst the amount ($) of aid is growing in absolute terms when measured as a percentage of donor country national incomes, it is in relative decline. Few countries (Denmark, Luxembourg, Netherlands, Norway and Sweden) have reached the OECD guideline of 0.7% of GNI. The USA donates around 0.2% of GNI.

- **Trade vs. aid**

The theoretical benefits of trade to ELDCs have already been outlined. Trade could expand export markets and enable a growth in incomes/revenues that can then be used to fund capital and human capital investment, and primary sectors may be able to access the benefits from economies of scale. Diversification may also be possible and enable ELDCs to access further export markets. Increases in income may then play a key role in reversing existing poverty cycles/traps. With increased incomes comes the possibility of a reduced reliance on aid.

However there are a number of significant barriers to such a process. Currently the USA and EU subsidise/protect their agricultural markets to a significant extent and this acts as a very effective barrier to 'free' trade in exactly the markets in which many ELDCs have a comparative advantage. ELDCs have had to also contend with falling commodity prices due to over-production by the subsidised US and EU economies. Freer trade would also result in many exceptions to WTO rules, which would have to be abandoned by ELDCs, and this would result in a competitive environment in which they would be at a distinct disadvantage.

- **The IMF**

The **IMF** aims to foster global monetary cooperation, secure financial stability, facilitate international trade, promote high levels of employment and sustainable economic growth, and reduce world poverty. IMF loans usually come with a package of policies, known as **stablisation policies**. These policies have meant that ELDC governments have been restricted in their use of **fiscal policy**. Government spending is restricted, and tax systems are reformed to collect revenue more effectively, be more progressive and counter tax avoidance/evasion by the wealthy. Most policies, focusing on reforming the structure of ELDC economies, are **supply-side** policies. Given the structure of these economies, an active demand management policy is hard to organise. Stabilisation programmes often impart a sharp shock to ELDC economies with which they are not able to cope. The tightening of domestic monetary and fiscal policies reduces aggregate demand leading to recession. The IMF 'blueprint' often fails to recognise the differences between individual countries and there are cases where countries that have followed a different path from that suggested by the IMF, have been able to develop just as well, if not better, than those following IMF advice. IMF decision-making is also dominated by rich countries.

- **The World Bank**

The **World Bank** attempted to encourage growth and development through loans for investment with accompanying advice and tight conditions for repayment. During the 1970s and 1980s **Structural adjustment programmes (SAPs)** caused many problems for the ELDCs associated with these two international institutions. Whilst targeting growth, programmes were criticised for causing de-development and so the bank now has much more of a focus on sustainable development as well as poverty alleviation and debt relief for poor countries.

More recently the World Bank has focused on sustainable development, the breaking of poverty cycles and the institutional reforms needed for the effective working of markets, for example:
- Health care and education provision
- Effective taxation systems
- Access to credit

- Property rights
- Empowerment of women
- Reduced corruption
- Infrastructure
- Innovation
- Political rights

As with the IMF, World Bank decision-making is dominated by rich countries and the scope of the changes advised can result in a 'loss of sovereignty' for many ELDCs. Tight conditions for ELDCs (tight fiscal and monetary policies and well as free trade) can seem very harsh for poor countries and often result in a widening income distribution.

INTERNATIONAL DEBT

● International finance

The debt problem has its roots back in the 1973/4 petrol price inflation and 'petrodollars' flooding banks in rich countries. Many of these banks loaned this inflow of funds to ELDCs who were importing oil and thus needed foreign exchange to help with their current account deficits. Debts involve huge servicing costs (both the principle loan and the interest payments) which have to be paid before anything else. **Debt** therefore severely hampers a country's attempts to develop, as income has to be used for debt repayment rather than investment in capital, human capital or social and economic infrastructure. A rescheduling of debts has often been accompanied by forced **structural reforms**. These reforms have been based upon **market forces**, **supply-side policies**, **deflationary fiscal** and **monetary policies** to target **inflation**, the reduction of government debt and the encouragement of exports by **devaluing** the currency. These reforms have often been a painful experience for many ELDCs, resulting in reduced welfare provision and widening **income distribution**.

The HIPC (Heavily Indebted Poor Country) Initiative along with the MDRI (Multilateral Debt Relief Initiative) both seek to provide debt relief to the most indebted ELDCs. Countries qualify if their GNI per capita is below a certain level and then they have to follow World Bank/IMF policies and use any 'savings' for poverty reduction.

ELDCs can also suffer problems by not being able to convert their domestic currency **(non-convertible currency)** for foreign currencies causing obvious problems for international trade.

Capital flight is a capital outflow from any country, but for ELDCs this can be a particular problem as valuable funds for investment resources move to another country.

MARKETS VS. INTERVENTION

- **Market-oriented policies**

Policies:
- Free trade
- Floating exchange rates
- Labour market reforms
- Deregulation and privatisation
- Liberalised flows of capital, goods and services

Strengths:
- Reduced incidence of government failure
- Efficient working of the price mechanism
- Competition and efficiency
- Allocative and productive efficiency from reduced barriers to entry and the movement of resources

Weaknesses:
- Market failure (externalities and merit goods especially)
- Asymmetric information in markets
- Weak/missing institutions needed for effective markets
- Income/access to resource and credit inequality
- Development of dual economy

- **Interventionist policies**

Policies:
- Provision of infrastructure
- State provided/subsidised education and health care
- Welfare safety nets
- Demand-side policies to maintain macro stability

Strengths:
- Correction of market failure
- Stable macro objectives
- Reduced income inequality and safety nets provided
- Infrastructure provision

Weaknesses:
- Government failure
- Red tape, bureaucracy and corruption
- Planning problems through lack of information and time-lags

- **Market with government intervention**

Good governance is key to balancing markets and intervention effectively, focusing on *how* rather than *what* policies are pursued. There are many examples of how intervention can work (health care, education and infrastructure) and there are many examples where markets work (export promotion, reduced trade barriers, privatisation). Whilst the poorest ELDCs can certainly benefit from initially more interventionist policies, a gradual withdrawal of government 'control' is seen as ideal. There is no 'blueprint' set of policies: all countries are unique, with different histories, resources endowments, different cultures and different circumstances.

DEVELOPMENT ECONOMICS SAMPLE QUESTIONS

Development Economics is examined in Paper 2 (data response) Section B.

1. (a) Define the following terms:

        (i)   Economic development   (2 marks)

        (ii)   Bilateral aid   (2 marks)

   (b) Explain how foreign aid can help a country to break out of a poverty cycle.   (4 marks)

   (c) With reference to [...], explain why there is a difference between the Human Development Index (HDI) figures for country A and country B.   (4 marks)

   (d) Using information from the text/data and your knowledge of economics, evaluate the effectiveness of aid in promoting economic development.   (8 marks)

Data responses are questions that are based upon text and data, which are not included here. There is more information on this with the model markschemes at the end of the book.

REVISION ADVICE

Whatever subject you are revising for, your aims, and to a certain extent, your methods, are the same. You are aiming to **learn your subject material**, and to **develop exam skills**.

Each person has to find the revision technique which works best for them. If you are in the final stages of your IB revision in the run-up to your exams you will probably have been able to try out some techniques already in your trial exams and will know whether they have worked for you or not. If they have *not* worked, then don't use them again. Try something different.

One of the dangers of just reading through your notes (apart from the fact that this tends to send even the most enthusiastic student to sleep) is that you will confuse understanding with memory. **Understanding and memory are different brain functions**. You understand your notes, but you can never be sure that you have actually acquired and internalised the information they contain. You must test your knowledge to be sure of this.

The good news is that this doesn't have to mean sitting through three-hour trial exam papers! To learn your material, you will have to go over it **again and again** (there is no substitute for this repetition: it's the way that your brain creates the neurological connections which constitute memory). Practise the techniques that you will be using in the exam: defining terms, drawing and explaining diagrams, brainstorming, essay plans (you **will** be doing essay plans in the exam!), graph drawing etc., all of which will enable you to **test your knowledge**, and **develop and practise exam skills** in an efficient timeframe. The most effective time period to revisit a chunk of material is between 20-30 minutes; any more and your brain's efficiency starts to decline (the law of diminishing marginal returns), and any less it doesn't have time to get into gear. In 20 minutes you can do two essay plans.

Always **start with what you know**. Say, for example, you are revising monopoly. Your first revision of this topic might start with a blank sheet of paper on which you write everything you can think of about monopoly. After you have spent 10 minutes on this, go back to your notes and see what you didn't know. Add this information to your brainstorm. The next time you revise this topic do, for example, three monopoly-based questions. Don't waste time actually writing them... just jot down a plan for them (don't forget the graphs), then go back to your notes once again and see what you forgot. You should remember more than the first time. Not only will you be testing your monopoly knowledge and *increasing* it as you go over the material for a second time, but you will be forcing yourself to plan, and almost best of all, you will be forced to write three *different* plans which answer the questions in a structured way, rather than writing your catch-all standard answer on monopoly. While it is difficult to predict what is going to come up on a paper, it's a certainty that you won't see a question inviting you to 'Write down everything you know about monopoly'. Your third revision of monopoly might see you writing out those short answers in full, or doing a couple of essay plans.

The key to making your revision work is to organise your time. **Make a revision plan**. This plan should divide the topics you need to revise into the total amount of time you have left before the exam. Don't wait: **do it today!** There's always less time than you think. Don't leave out this important stage in the revision process: you might be working away happily thinking you are accomplishing a great deal, without a sense of how much you are effectively getting covered. Plan to cover each topic at least three times, and include in your plan the method you are going to use to cover the material, whether a brainstorm, getting a really full set of notes, doing two essay plans and two data-response plans.

This method helps to **calm exam fears**. As you progress through your revision plan, you will have positive proof your knowledge is improving as you revisit each topic. You will **know** your revision is working. You will be in control of the process, and will be focusing on small, manageable tasks rather than a gigantic formless mass of syllabus material. Almost everyone will be worried about their upcoming exams, no matter what grade they will get. Just because you are worried does *not* mean that you are not going to do well.

With a structured set of notes, a realistic revision plan and some good old-fashioned graft, you can do well. Probably better than you think! I wish you all the very best of luck with your revision, and with your exam.

ASSESSMENT OBJECTIVES (AOS)

These assessment objectives give candidates a clear indication of the type and level of skill required for each section of the syllabus and in each type of assessment. You should use them as a guide to the depth of understanding and the types of skills you need to develop for each idea and concept.

AO1: Demonstrate knowledge and understanding.
For example:
- Definitions in part (a) of essays
- Definitions in (a) parts (i) and (ii) of data responses

AO2: Demonstrate application and analysis of knowledge and understanding.
For example:
- Explaining appropriate diagrams in parts (b) and (c) of data responses.

- Developing explanations of theory in part (a) of essays.

AO3: Demonstrate synthesis and evaluation.
For example:
- Part (b) of essays.
- Part (d) of data responses.

AO4: Select, use and apply a variety of appropriate skills and techniques.
For example:
- Selecting the appropriate diagrams in parts (b) and (c) of data responses.
- Selection of mathematical techniques in HL paper 3.

HIGHER LEVEL ASSESSMENT

External assessment (4 hours)	80%

Paper 1 (1 hour 30 minutes) Essay paper	30%

AOs 1, 2, 3 and 4
50 marks

Divided into two sections. Candidates have to answer one question from each section.

There is a choice of two questions in each section. Each essay is marked out of 25 marks, with 10 marks for part (a) and 15 marks for part (b).

Section A
Microeconomics (Syllabus section 1)

Section B
Macroeconomics (Syllabus section 2)

Paper 2 (1 hour 30 minutes) Data response paper	30%

AOs 1, 2, 3 and 4
40 marks

Divided into two sections and candidates have to answer one question from each section.

There is a choice of two questions in each section. Each data response is marked out of 20 marks (2, 2, 4, 4, 8 for each subsection in turn).

Section A
International economics (Syllabus section 3)

Section B
Development economics (Syllabus section 4)

Paper 3 (1 hour) **HL extension paper (quantitative techniques)**	**20%**

AOs 1, 2 and 4
50 marks

Candidates answer two questions from a choice of three (25 marks per question).

This paper is based on all the HL extension material throughout all four sections of the syllabus, and focuses on the mathematical elements of the course.

Internal assessment (4 hours)	**20%**

AOs 1, 2, 3 and 4
45 marks

A portfolio of three commentaries (20 teaching hours) internally assessed by teachers and externally moderated by the IB at the end of the course.

Each commentary (max 750 words) is marked out of 14 with 3 marks, overall, for the rubric requirements.

ESSAY TECHNIQUE

The problem with giving model answers for essays in this kind of revision guide is that one has to be provided for each area of the syllabus, and space constraints prevent this here. If you are getting together to revise with friends, you might want to compare essays you have done in the past, looking carefully at where your teacher has indicated good and bad practice, and where marks have been indicated in the margin, as well as comments for your future improvement. One surprisingly effective thing to do is to mark each others' essays, using the readily available markschemes. This will give you a real insight into what points actually constitute marks.

There is a danger of pre-learning answers to essays in one's revision, resulting in generalised, unfocused and unstructured answers in an exam. The suggestions offered on the use of essay planning in one's revision in the revision advice section above will help you to avoid this pitfall.

Examiners often comment on candidates who do not **separate the two parts of essays**. The markscheme the examiner is working with instructs him or her to award marks specifically in each part of the question. If your answer to a two-part question consists of one undifferentiated answer, your examiner will struggle to apply the markscheme. It is also something which is calculated to annoy your examiner! Another frequent cause of lost marks is to provide information in part (a) which should really be in part (b). Careful planning (practised in your revision) will solve this problem entirely.

Well-planned and written essays will **address the command words** of the question (eg. "Explain...", "Discuss..."). If you are not sure about the precise meanings of the various command words, then your revision period is your chance to find out. Good sources of this information are to be found in the IBO Economics Guide.

I have placed much emphasis on the use of **diagrams** in all your work. Marks are available in your examiner's markscheme for your graphs. In essays they must be clearly drawn and accurately labelled and fully integrated into the text ('in the diagram below...' 'this is shown in the diagram below...'). Weak candidates do not use diagrams, and if they do, they are messy, incorrectly labelled, hard to read, contain wrongly-positioned curves and are sometimes irrelevant to the question.

MODEL MARKSCHEMES

Section A (Microeconomics)

1. (a) **Explain the importance of cross elasticity of demand and price elasticity of demand for firms when making decisions.**

Answers should include:
*   A definition of XED
*   A definition of PED
*   The link between the demand for a good and changes in the prices of complements and substitutes
*   The link between price changes, total revenue and PED
*   Real-life examples to illustrate the above

Answers may include:
*   Use of diagrams to illustrate PED and total revenue
*   Use of diagrams to illustrate complement/substitute relationships
*   Explanation that both XED and PED are both hard to measure accurately

(a)   **10 marks**

Examiners should be aware that candidates may take a different approach which if appropriate, should be rewarded.

Level		Marks
0	*Completely inappropriate answer*	*0*
1	*Little understanding of the specific demands of the question* *Very little recognition of relevant economic theory* *Relevant terms not defined* *Significant errors*	*1–3*
2	*Some understanding of the specific demands of the question* *Some recognition of relevant economic theory* *Some relevant terms defined* *Some errors*	*4–6*
3	*Understanding of the specific demands of the question* *Relevant economic theory explained and developed* *Relevant economic terms defined* *Few errors* *Where appropriate, diagrams included*	*7-8*
4	*Clear understanding of the specific demands of the question* *Relevant economic theory clearly explained and developed* *Relevant economic terms clearly defined* *No major errors* *Where appropriate, diagrams included and explained* *Where appropriate, examples used*	*9-10*

(b) Studies have shown that the demand for petrol tends to be highly price inelastic. Evaluate a policy of substantially raising taxes on petrol as a method of reducing its consumption.

Answers may include:

- Petrol as an example of market failure
- Use of MSC/MSB diagram to illustrate market failure
- Inelastic demand and the implications for a tax on petrol (PED<1 may result in a proportionately small decrease in quantity demanded of petrol)
- Size of tax increase that may be needed to have a substantial impact
- Incidence of tax
- Problem of Tax=MSC
- Impact of government tax revenue
- Assessment of alternative policies

(b)   **15 marks**

Effective evaluation may be to:
    consider short-term versus long-term consequences
    examine the impact on different stakeholders
    discuss advantages and disadvantages
    prioritize the arguments.

Examiners should be aware that candidates may take a different approach which if appropriate, should be rewarded.

Level		Marks
0	Completely inappropriate answer	0
1	Little understanding of the specific demands of the question Very little recognition of relevant economic theory Relevant terms not defined Significant errors	1–5
2	Some understanding of the specific demands of the question Some recognition of relevant economic theory Some relevant terms defined Some errors	6-9
3	Understanding of the specific demands of the question Relevant economic theory explained and developed Relevant economic terms defined Few errors Where appropriate, diagrams included An attempt at evaluation	10-12
4	Clear understanding of the specific demands of the question Relevant economic theory clearly explained and developed Relevant economic terms clearly defined No major errors Where appropriate, diagrams included and explained Where appropriate, examples used Evidence of appropriate evaluation	13-15

2. (a) **Using diagrams, explain the difference between a perfectly competitive firm, in terms of profits, in the short-run and the long-run.**

    Answers <u>should</u> include:
    - Definitions of abnormal and normal profits
    - An outline of perfect competition
    - Short-run perfect competition diagram showing abnormal profit at the profit maximising output level
    - Explanation of new firms/resources entering (attracted by abnormal profits), market supply increasing resulting in price falling and normal profits in the long-run

    Answers <u>may</u> include:
    - Microeconomics distinction between short and long run
    - Further explanation of why abnormal profits are made
    - Further diagrams to explain the movement of the firm from short to long-run equilibrium

(a)   10 marks

Examiners should be aware that candidates may take a different approach which if appropriate, should be rewarded.

Level		Marks
0	Completely inappropriate answer	0
1	Little understanding of the specific demands of the question Very little recognition of relevant economic theory Relevant terms not defined Significant errors	1–3
2	Some understanding of the specific demands of the question Some recognition of relevant economic theory Some relevant terms defined Some errors	4–6
3	Understanding of the specific demands of the question Relevant economic theory explained and developed Relevant economic terms defined Few errors Where appropriate, diagrams included	7-8
4	Clear understanding of the specific demands of the question Relevant economic theory clearly explained and developed Relevant economic terms clearly defined No major errors Where appropriate, diagrams included and explained Where appropriate, examples used	9-10

(b) Evaluate the view that perfect competition is a more desirable market structure than monopoly.

Answers _may_ include:
- An explanation of the difference between perfect competition and monopoly
- Diagrams to illustrate the two market structure
- Explanation of "desirable" in terms of different stakeholders
- Comparison in terms of: allocative/productive efficiency, dynamic efficiency in the long run, price/output/profits, choice for consumers, barriers to entry, non-price competition, research and development, benefits from economies of scale etc
- An assessment of which market structure is most desirable

(b)   15 marks

Effective evaluation may be to:
consider short-term versus long-term consequences
examine the impact on different stakeholders
discuss advantages and disadvantages
prioritize the arguments.

Examiners should be aware that candidates may take a different approach which if appropriate, should be rewarded.

Level		Marks
0	Completely inappropriate answer	0
1	Little understanding of the specific demands of the question Very little recognition of relevant economic theory Relevant terms not defined Significant errors	1–5
2	Some understanding of the specific demands of the question Some recognition of relevant economic theory Some relevant terms defined Some errors	6-9
3	Understanding of the specific demands of the question Relevant economic theory explained and developed Relevant economic terms defined Few errors Where appropriate, diagrams included An attempt at evaluation	10-12
4	Clear understanding of the specific demands of the question Relevant economic theory clearly explained and developed Relevant economic terms clearly defined No major errors Where appropriate, diagrams included and explained Where appropriate, examples used Evidence of appropriate evaluation	13-15

Section B (Macroeconomics)

1.   (a) **Explain why a country may wish to reduce its inflation rate.**

Answers <u>should</u> include:
- An explanation of the rate of inflation
- An explanation of the causes of inflation
- An explanation of the reason to reduce inflation in terms of the various costs of inflation. This <u>may</u> include the impact of competitiveness, the price mechanism, redistribution of incomes, devaluing incomes, confidence etc

(a)   10 marks

Examiners should be aware that candidates may take a different approach which if appropriate, should be rewarded.

Level		Marks
0	*Completely inappropriate answer*	*0*
1	*Little understanding of the specific demands of the question* *Very little recognition of relevant economic theory* *Relevant terms not defined* *Significant errors*	*1–3*
2	*Some understanding of the specific demands of the question* *Some recognition of relevant economic theory* *Some relevant terms defined* *Some errors*	*4–6*
3	*Understanding of the specific demands of the question* *Relevant economic theory explained and developed* *Relevant economic terms defined* *Few errors* *Where appropriate, diagrams included*	*7-8*
4	*Clear understanding of the specific demands of the question* *Relevant economic theory clearly explained and developed* *Relevant economic terms clearly defined* *No major errors* *Where appropriate, diagrams included and explained* *Where appropriate, examples used*	*9-10*

(b) **Evaluate the likely effects on an economy of relying on demand-side policies to reduce the rate of inflation.**

Answers may include:
- An explanation of fiscal and monetary policies to reduce inflation
- Linkages to AD
- Use of AD and AS diagrams to illustrate
- An explanation of the suitability of demand side policies for demand-pull inflation
- Strengths and weaknesses of fiscal policies
- Strengths and weaknesses of monetary policies
- The impact on output, growth, employment and balance of payments and possible policy conflicts/trade-offs
- Cost-push inflation and the effectiveness of demand-side policies
- Alternative supply-side policies
- Inflation targeting

(b) **15 marks**

Effective evaluation may be to:
consider short-term versus long-term consequences
examine the impact on different stakeholders
discuss advantages and disadvantages
prioritize the arguments.

Examiners should be aware that candidates may take a different approach which if appropriate, should be rewarded.

Level		Marks
0	*Completely inappropriate answer*	0
1	*Little understanding of the specific demands of the question* *Very little recognition of relevant economic theory* *Relevant terms not defined* *Significant errors*	1–5
2	*Some understanding of the specific demands of the question* *Some recognition of relevant economic theory* *Some relevant terms defined* *Some errors*	6-9
3	*Understanding of the specific demands of the question* *Relevant economic theory explained and developed* *Relevant economic terms defined* *Few errors* *Where appropriate, diagrams included* *An attempt at evaluation*	10-12
4	*Clear understanding of the specific demands of the question* *Relevant economic theory clearly explained and developed* *Relevant economic terms clearly defined* *No major errors* *Where appropriate, diagrams included and explained* *Where appropriate, examples used* *Evidence of appropriate evaluation*	13-15

2. **(a) Explain how fiscal policy can be used to make supply-side improvements to an economy.**

Answers should include:
- Definition of fiscal policy
- Explanation of "supply-side" improvements
- Use of AD/AS concepts and diagrams
- Explanation of how government spending may be used to affect LRAS (eg. reduced spending on benefits, increased spending on health care and education)
- Explanation of how taxes may be used to affect LRAS (eg. reduced direct taxation to improve incentives to work, lower corporation tax to incentivise investment, reduced costs of production through lower indirect taxes)

(a)   *10 marks*

Examiners should be aware that candidates may take a different approach which if appropriate, should be rewarded.

Level		Marks
0	Completely inappropriate answer	0
1	Little understanding of the specific demands of the question Very little recognition of relevant economic theory Relevant terms not defined Significant errors	1–3
2	Some understanding of the specific demands of the question Some recognition of relevant economic theory Some relevant terms defined Some errors	4–6
3	Understanding of the specific demands of the question Relevant economic theory explained and developed Relevant economic terms defined Few errors Where appropriate, diagrams included	7-8
4	Clear understanding of the specific demands of the question Relevant economic theory clearly explained and developed Relevant economic terms clearly defined No major errors Where appropriate, diagrams included and explained Where appropriate, examples used	9-10

(b) **Evaluate the use of supply-side policies to increase real Gross Domestic Product (GDP).**

Answers *may* include:
- A definition of real GDP
- A definition of supply-side policies
- Examples of supply-side policies to be used
- A distinction between interventionist and market oriented policies
- AD/AS diagrams to illustrate and increase in real GDP
- Distinction between growth of actual and potential output
- Benefits of using supply-side policies (eg. reduced inflation pressure, long-term approach)
- Problems of applying supply-side policies to increase real GDP (eg. time lag, impact on equity, interventionist policies and government budget)

(b)   *15 marks*

Effective evaluation may be to:
        consider short-term versus long-term consequences
        examine the impact on different stakeholders
        discuss advantages and disadvantages
        prioritize the arguments.

Examiners should be aware that candidates may take a different approach which if appropriate, should be rewarded.

Level		Marks
0	*Completely inappropriate answer*	0
1	*Little understanding of the specific demands of the question* *Very little recognition of relevant economic theory* *Relevant terms not defined* *Significant errors*	*1–5*
2	*Some understanding of the specific demands of the question* *Some recognition of relevant economic theory* *Some relevant terms defined* *Some errors*	*6-9*
3	*Understanding of the specific demands of the question* *Relevant economic theory explained and developed* *Relevant economic terms defined* *Few errors* *Where appropriate, diagrams included* *An attempt at evaluation*	*10-12*
4	*Clear understanding of the specific demands of the question* *Relevant economic theory clearly explained and developed* *Relevant economic terms clearly defined* *No major errors* *Where appropriate, diagrams included and explained* *Where appropriate, examples used* *Evidence of appropriate evaluation*	*13-15*

DATA RESPONSE TECHNIQUE

Choose the question by reading all of the individual question parts, especially those with the most marks. **Allocate the time you spend on the different parts of the question according to the distribution of the marks**. You should spend double the amount of time on an 8-mark question than you spend on a 4-mark question. This sounds obvious, but a number of students will misallocate their resources each year with catastrophic results. Make sure that you are not one of them!

Data response answers **must be planned** like any good essay. Use both the text and the data available to you to illustrate your answers.

The opening questions will require you to be able to provide definitions of key terms in the text. The next questions will often ask you to use a diagram to explain either an event described in the text or to explain a specific piece of theory that is applicable to the text. The final question will require you to analyse and evaluate an issue based upon the text, and as these are most difficult skills needed in the exam this question is awarded 8/20 marks. If you are to perform well in this paper, then you must seek to maximise your marks on this question. If you can maximise the number of marks you gain from the define/describe/explain questions (questions (a), (b) and (c) give you potentially 12/20 marks) then 4/8 in part (d) will give you 16/20 marks (80%).

Part (a)
2-4 lines will be sufficient to gain full marks on this question. You will need to make at least two points to gain full marks.

Parts (b) and (c)
There are 2 marks for the diagram, and 2 marks for your writing about the diagram. Diagrams must be fully labelled. Watch out for details that matter (eg. an *ad valorem* tax should be illustrated by a divergent shift of the supply curve). Your written explanation of the diagram should describe *what* has happened in the diagram, and explain *why* it has happened.

Part (d)
Making clear use of the text (actually quote and state which paragraph is being quoted) is necessary to gain more than 5 out of 8 marks. Your answer must be based upon economic concepts and the development of concepts, rather than simply quoting from the text.

Evaluation should look at different stakeholders (consumers, producers, employees, government, community, the environment and other countries), short- versus long-run, prioritise arguments and must always be set in the context of the text/data.

MODEL MARKSCHEMES

Section A (International Economics)

(a) *Define the following terms indicated in bold in the text:*

(i) **Exchange rate** *(2 marks)*

Level		Marks
0	*Wrong definition*	0
1	*Vague definition* How much a currency is worth.	1
2	*Precise definition* It is the price (or value) of one currency expressed or converted in terms of another. An example is not required	2

(ii) **Appreciation** *(2 marks)*

Level		Marks
0	*Wrong definition*	0
1	*Vague definition* A currency becomes more expensive.	1
2	*Precise definition* It is an increase in the value (or price) of one currency in terms of another currency in a floating exchange rate system.	2

(b) **Using an appropriate diagram, explain how increased spending on food imports could affect an exchange rate.**
(4 marks)

Level		Marks
0	*Inappropriate answer*	0
1	*Identification of appropriate theory* For drawing a correctly-labelled exchange rate diagram showing how an increase in spending on food imports results in an increase in the supply of the currency on the foreign exchange market and a fall in the value of the currency, ceteris paribus **or** an explanation that the increased purchase of food imports would lead to an increase in the supply of the currency on the foreign exchange market and a fall in the value of a currency, ceteris paribus.	1-2
2	*Correct application of appropriate theory* For drawing a correctly labelled exchange rate diagram	3-4

<table>
<tr>
<td></td>
<td>showing how an increase in spending on food imports results in an increase in the supply of the currency on the foreign exchange market and a fall in the value of the currency, ceteris paribus **and** an explanation that the increased purchase of food imports would lead to an increase in the supply of the currency on the foreign exchange market and a fall in the value of the currency, ceteris paribus.</td>
<td></td>
</tr>
</table>

A diagram showing and explaining a fall in demand for a currency and so a depreciation may receive a maximum of (1 mark) for the diagram, and (0 marks) for the explanation.

Candidates who incorrectly label diagrams can be rewarded with a maximum of (3 marks).

The vertical axis may be price (or value) of the currency in US$ (or in other currencies), US$/currency or exchange rate. The horizontal axis should be quantity of currency or just quantity (or Q). *A title is not necessary.*

(c) **Using an appropriate diagram, explain how the continuing increase in prices for imported raw materials could affect the general price level and output.** (4 marks)

Level		Marks
0	*Inappropriate answer*	*0*
1	*Identification of appropriate theory* For drawing a correctly labelled AD/AS diagram showing a decrease in AS **or** an explanation of how increased raw material prices increase production costs, shifting AS and contributing to a higher price level and lower output.	*1-2*
2	*Correct application of appropriate theory* For drawing a correctly labelled AD/AS diagram showing a decrease in AS **and** an explanation of how increased raw material prices increase production costs, shifting AS and contributing to a higher price level and lower output.	*3-4*

Candidates who incorrectly label diagrams can receive a maximum of (3 marks).

For AD/AS, the vertical axis may be price level, average price level, or inflation. The horizontal axis may be output, real output, national output, real national output, national income (Y), or GDP. Any appropriate abbreviations, such as APL, CPI, RNO or RNY are allowable. A title is not necessary.

(d) Using information from the text/data and your knowledge of economics, evaluate the impact on an economy of the decision to introduce tariffs. (8 marks)

Responses may include:
- A definition of tariffs
- A tariff diagram
- Revenue from tariffs could help reduce the budget deficit
- Tariffs on imported goods will discourage their purchase and so less imports will reduce the current account deficit
- Tariffs will encourage production in domestic import-competing industries
- Tariffs can protect and encourage employment in domestic industries
- Tariffs contribute to a dead-weight loss of welfare, because of the loss of consumer surplus
- Tariffs lead to an inefficient allocation of resources, because goods are produced by relatively inefficient domestic producers as opposed to more efficient foreign producers
- Tariffs can have an inflationary impact in a country tariffs could encourage producers to diversify and avoid the risk of over-specialization
- Introduction of tariffs may result in retaliation which may affect export industries making it difficult to achieve export-led growth
- Tariffs may go against WTO rules

Examiners should be aware that candidates may take a different approach which if appropriate, should be rewarded.

If there is no direct reference to the text/data, then candidates may not be rewarded beyond level 2.

Effective evaluation may be to:
- *consider short-term versus long-term consequences*
- *examine the impact on different stakeholders*
- *discuss advantages and disadvantages*
- *prioritize the arguments.*

Level		Marks
0	No valid discussion	0
1	Few relevant concepts recognized. Little discussion or only basic understanding.	1-2
2	Relevant concepts recognized and developed in reasonable depth Some attempt at application and analysis.	3-5
3	Relevant concepts developed in reasonable depth, demonstrating effective evaluation, supported by appropriate evidence or theory.	6-8

Section B (Development economics)

(a) *Define the following terms indicated in bold in the text:*

(i) Economic development
(2 marks)

Level		Marks
0	*Wrong definition*	0
1	*Vague definition* The idea that living standards improve.	1

2	*Precise definition*
	
	It is a broad concept involving any two of the following:
	       · improvement in living standards
	       · reduction in poverty
	       · improved education and health
	       · reduction in unemployment
	       · greater equality in income distribution
	       · environmental protection
	       · increased freedom
		2

(ii) Bilateral aid
(2 marks)

Level		Marks
0	*Wrong definition*	0
1	*Vague definition* Two countries are involved in aid.	1
2	*Precise definition* Aid that is given directly from one country to another.	2

(b) Explain how foreign aid can help a country to break out of a poverty cycle.
(4 marks)

Level		Marks
0	*Inappropriate answer*	0
1	*Identification of appropriate theory* An explanation of a poverty cycle (eg. low incomes ⇨ low savings ⇨ low investment ⇨ leading to low incomes etc.) **or** that foreign aid can increase resources available in the economy, leading to higher incomes etc.	1-2
2	*Correct application of appropriate theory* An explanation of a poverty cycle (eg. low incomes ⇨ to low savings ⇨ low investment ⇨ leading to low incomes etc.) **and** that foreign aid can increase resources available in the economy, leading to higher incomes etc.	3-4

N.B. An alternative poverty cycle may be used, and if appropriately explained, may be fully rewarded. Candidates may also explain a break in a poverty cycle in a different way and if appropriately explained, this approach may be fully rewarded.

(c) With reference to the text, explain why there is a difference between the Human Development Index (HDI) figures for country A and country B.   (4 marks)

Level		Marks
0	*Inappropriate answer*	*0*
1	*Identification of appropriate theory* For noting that one country has a higher HDI than the other and that HDI includes other factors than just GDP per capita.	*1-2*
2	*Correct application of appropriate theory* For noting that one country has a higher HDI than the other and that HDI includes other factors than just GDP. For full marks comments on health care and education. In comparison to GDP per capita figures would be needed.	*3-4*

(d) Using information from the text/data and your knowledge of economics, evaluate the effectiveness of aid in promoting economic development.   (8 marks)

Responses may include:
- Discussion of types of aid, eg. multi-lateral/bilateral, tied etc.
- A comparison of official aid and unofficial aid.
- Benefits of aid which is targeted to meeting development objective
- Aid can contribute to economic growth which might then be used to achieve development objectives
- Benefits of cooperation between aid agencies and other agencies and groups (eg. governments and local communities)
- Benefits of aid driven by the needs of the people
- Benefits of aid linked to appropriate domestic policies and good governance
- Problems associated with aid (eg. corruption and dependency)

N.B. To reach level 3, candidates must direct their responses to the issue of promoting economic development, rather than write in general terms about aid.

Examiners should be aware that candidates may take a different approach which if appropriate, should be rewarded.

If there is no direct reference to the text/data, then candidates may not be rewarded beyond level 2.

Effective evaluation may be to:
- consider short-term versus long-term consequences
- examine the impact on different stakeholders
- discuss advantages and disadvantages
- prioritize the arguments.

Level		Marks
0	No valid discussion	0
1	Few relevant concepts recognized. Little discussion or only basic understanding.	1–2
2	Relevant concepts recognized and developed in reasonable depth Some attempt at application and analysis.	3-5
3	Relevant concepts developed in reasonable depth, demonstrating effective evaluation, supported by appropriate evidence or theory.	6-8

These 'outline' answers are structured in exactly the same format as the markschemes used by the IB. The 'generic' markschemes (showing the levels and marks in *italics* are taken from past paper markschemes and the Economics Guide).

IBDP REVISION COURSES

Summary

Who are they for?
Students about to take their final IBDP exams (May or November)

Locations include:
Oxford, UK
Rome, Italy
Brussels, Belgium
Dubai, UAE
Adelaide, Sydney & Melbourne, AUS
Munich, Germany

Duration
2.5 days per subject
Students can take multiple subjects

The most successful IB revision courses worldwide

Highly-experienced IB teachers and examiners

Every class is tailored to the needs of that particular group of students

Features

- Classes grouped by grade (UK)
- Exam skills and techniques – typical traps identified
- Exam practice
- Pre-course online questionnaire to identify problem areas
- Small groups of 8–10 students
- 24-hour pastoral care.

Revising for the final IB exams without expert guidance is tough. Students attending OSC Revision Courses get more work done in a shorter time than they could possibly have imagined.

With a different teacher, who is confident in their subject and uses their experience and expertise to explain new approaches and exam techniques, students rapidly improve their understanding. OSC's teaching team consists of examiners and teachers with years of experience – they have the knowledge and skills students need to get top grades.

The size of our Oxford course gives some particular advantages to students. With over 1,000 students and 300 classes, we can group students by grade – enabling them to go at a pace that suits them.

Students work hard, make friends and leave OSC feeling invigorated and confident about their final exams.

We understand the needs of IBDP students – our decades of experience, hand-picked teachers and intense atmosphere can improve your grades.

> **I got 40 points overall, two points up from my prediction of 38, and up 7 points from what I had been scoring in my mocks over the years, before coming to OSC. Thank you so much for all your help!**
>
> OSC Student

Please note that locations and course features are subject to change - please check our website for up-to-date details.

Find out more: 🏠 osc-ib.com/revision 📱 +44 (0)1865 512802

MID IBDP SUMMER PROGRAMMES

Summary

Who is it for?
For students entering their final year of the IB Diploma Programme

Locations include:
Harvard and MIT, USA
Cambridge, UK

Duration
Min. 1 week, max. 6 weeks
1 or 2 IB subjects per week

Improve confidence and grades

Highly-experienced IB teachers and examiners

Tailored classes to meet students' needs

Wide range of available subjects

Safe accommodation and 24-hour pastoral care

Features

- Morning teaching in chosen IB subject
- 2nd IB subject afternoon classes
- IB Skills afternoon classes
- One-to-one Extended Essay Advice, Private Tuition and University Guidance options
- Small classes
- Daily homework
- Unique IB university fair
- Class reports for parents
- Full social programme.

By the end of their first year, students understand the stimulating and challenging nature of the IB Diploma.

They also know that the second year is crucial in securing the required grades to get into their dream college or university.

This course helps students to avoid a 'summer dip' by using their time effectively. With highly-experienced IB teachers, we consolidate a student's year one

learning, close knowledge gaps, and introduce some year two material.

In a relaxed environment, students develop academically through practice revision and review. They are taught new skills, techniques, and perspectives – giving a real boost to their grades. This gives students an enormous amount of confidence and drive for their second year.

> "The whole experience was incredible. The university setting was inspiring, the friends I made, and the teaching was first-class. I feel so much more confident in myself and in my subject.
>
> OSC Student

Please note that locations and course features are subject to change - please check our website for up-to-date details.

Find out more: osc-ib.com/mid +44 (0)1865 512802